Supporting Student Transitions 14–19

Supporting Student Transitions 14–19 offers transition focused approaches to planning, teaching, learning and assessment designed to meet the needs of these unique learners. Drawing upon the latest research and theory, as well as the authors' extensive experience in the field, it examines in detail transitions in teaching and learning in this complex sector.

Drawing out and critically analysing the key features of both pedagogy and andragogy, the book presents the best elements of each to provide all tutors and practitioners involved in the teaching of 14–19 learners with clear strategies for supporting this group. Practical advice backed by sound theory will provide readers with a clear understanding of the requirements and needs of learners in the school, college and university. Topics explored include:

- the role of the teacher in supporting student transitions;
- understanding transition focused approaches;
- emotional and social factors involved;
- recognising difficulties and helping students prepare.

Supporting Student Transitions 14–19 is a practical guide also offering a unique contribution to the discourse on this important sector of education, increasingly afforded the attention it deserves. It will be an essential resource for trainee teachers, students of FET, lecturers and teachers wanting to build upon their understanding of this group of learners.

John Bostock is Senior Lecturer in Teaching and Learning Development at Edge Hill University, UK

Jane Wood is Assistant Head of Further Education and Training at Edge Hill University, UK

Supporting Student Transitions 14–19

Approaches to teaching and learning

John Bostock and Jane Wood

Routledge
Taylor & Francis Group

LONDON AND NEW YORK

First published 2015
by Routledge
2 Park Square, Milton Park, Abingdon, Oxon OX14 4RN

and by Routledge
711 Third Avenue, New York, NY 10017

Routledge is an imprint of the Taylor & Francis Group, an informa business

British Library Cataloguing in Publication Data
A catalogue record for this book is available from the British Library

Library of Congress Cataloging in Publication Data
Bostock, John, 1962
  Supporting student transitions 14–19 : approaches to teaching and learning / John Bostock, Jane Wood.
  ISBN 978-0-415-82286-2 (hardback) — ISBN 978-0-415-82287-9 (paperback) — ISBN 978-1-315-76307-1 (e-book) 1. Education, Secondary. 2. College preparation programs. 3. School-to-work transition. 4. Educational sociology. I. Wood, Jane, 1963– II. Title.
  LA222.B66 2014
  373.1102—dc23
                                                    2014004876

ISBN: 978-0-415-82286-2 (hbk)
ISBN: 978-0-415-82287-9 (pbk)
ISBN: 978-1-315-76307-1 (ebk)

Typeset in Sabon
by Keystroke, Station Road, Codsall, Wolverhampton

Printed and bound in Great Britain by
TJ International Ltd, Padstow, Cornwall

Jane dedicates this book to her beautiful children and grandchildren who inspire and motivate her

Rachel, Catherine, Nicky, Alex and Daisy

John dedicates this to his nieces and nephew who always support and inspire him through the challenging moments

Rebecca, Helen, Elisabeth, Erica and Joshua

Contents

List of illustrations

Tables

Figures

Forewords

A considerable number of students attending schools and colleges often originate from a range of unpromising and challenging backgrounds. This is particularly pertinent to the age range of 14–19 where students are expected to have a clear vision for their current and future learning needs irrespective of the social and educational background that may have influenced them. This book successfully addresses a realistic variety of transitional approaches that encourage the teacher to consider the needs of the young adult in an holistic manner, ultimately resulting in successful achievement. This text combines experience with research to provide a particularly useful reference for both intending and practising teachers.

Margaret Postance
Head of Further Education and Training
Edge Hill University, UK

Consideration of 'Transitions' should always be a core component of curriculum planning for Learning and Professional Development. Equipping individuals to understand what is coming next and how to successfully navigate the future is not only essential to their success but it is a fair and ethical thing to do. This publication has this consideration at the heart of its ethos and the authors have focused clearly on the power of modelling, scaffolding and metacognition in the deployment of effective teaching for learning. In short, using real examples, they empower trainee teachers and teacher educators to be clearer about what transitions are and what transition experiences look and feel like in practice. Thus they offer an enhanced conceptual grasp of issues and practical solutions grounded in a structure that can be used to stimulate debate and dialogue. This makes the book profoundly developmental and one which has the potential to make a difference to the experiences and practice of all its readers.

Professor Mark Schofield
Dean of Teaching and Learning Development,
National Teaching Fellow
Edge Hill University, UK

Preface

For a long time the age range of 14–19 has been a significant time of transformation and transition in the lives of young people as they move from school to college or work and from school/college to university or work.

These transitions are often very difficult as young people are moved from known secure environments to new and challenging contexts. They may struggle to find their place in the new – often bigger – setting and may become isolated and troubled.

Our role is to understand these difficulties and to help and prepare students for transition periods and support them through changes to both their identities and their social/learning environment; to help them to be able to fit in smoothly and quickly and to maximise their learning and optimise their life chances, enabling them to move on as mature, independent, autonomous learners who are fully equipped for the world of work and are actively engaged citizens ready to take their place in society.

This book is based on our own experiences in the sector together with our own research. It has its foundation in real-life practical experience and knowledge.

We envisage the book as a simple source of reference and a guide to assist trainee or new teachers, whether in schools or colleges, to undertake teaching responsibilities with 14–19 year old learners with confidence and pride.

The book is split into two parts. Part 1 considers the emotional and social context and the role of teachers in supporting, mentoring and coaching young people to make successful transitions in their educational journeys. Part 2 considers the academic journey from pedagogy to andragogy and provides help and advice for teachers in making this transition for their students.

We have been very lucky in our careers to have had the privilege of working with students from all backgrounds and age ranges and have learnt so much from these young people and from the colleagues who have supported us throughout our careers.

We are very lucky to have the opportunity to be part of young people's lives at such transition periods, and this responsibility is taken very seriously.

They deserve the very best opportunity to embrace learning and to proceed onwards to become lifelong learners and active citizens in our society. They also deserve the very best teachers to support them on that journey.

Those teachers are yourselves, so please remember it is a huge honour and a massive responsibility – but most of all it is the best fun so relax and enjoy it!

Jane & John

Acknowledgements

We would like to thank David Ryan for all his help and support in editing and formatting this book.

We would especially like to thank the following colleagues and experts for their invaluable contributions:

Jacqui Basquill – Edge Hill University
Dawne Bell – Edge Hill University
Joanne Bostock – NHS
Myrtle Chadderton – Trafford College
Keith Cook – Edge Hill University
Hazel Devereux – Edge Hill University
Liz Diamond – Edge Hill University
Derek Doherty – Adult Community
Stu Field – Edge Hill University
Sarah Hamilton – Trafford College
Janet Harland – Trafford College
Anna Hartley – Trainee Teacher, Edge Hill University
Mark Hughes – West Lancashire College
Jane Martin – Shrewsbury College of Arts and Technology
Nuria Lleras Monks – St John Rigby College
Janie Morgan-Wood – Leicester College
Tony Thomas Morrison – International School, Qatar
Genevieve Parkes – University of Portsmouth
Cristina Pinon – Trafford College
Sally Ryan – York Steiner School
Dave Southworth – Wigan and Leigh College
Anthony Turjansky – Edge Hill University
David Wooff – Edge Hill University

Part 1

Relationships

Chapter 1

Introduction

New approaches to transition phases

Introduction

This introduction considers a transitions-focused approach to teaching 14–19 year olds and identifies why it is essential for teachers to manage the transition from school to college and from college to university for their students. This chapter will promote an understanding of these transitions-focused approaches and their relevance in improving learning, teaching, assessment, retention and achievement in these crucial transition phases.

We strongly believe that transitions involve much more than the move from one physical location to another or an age transition from one school to another. We suggest that transitions are profound periods of change and transformation in the lives of students and as such should be studied and managed to ensure students are able to grow and thrive during these difficult phases in their education. For the purposes of this book we use the term transition to mean the process of changing from one educational establishment to another, engendering a period of personal growth while facing challenges and demands, and where the chance to become a new person can be exploited. We do not believe that transitions are always negative experiences and we propose that they need not be troubled or problematic. With the help and support of teachers and support staff at both institutions, they can be a positive experience of challenge, growth and achievement.

Crafter and Maunder (2012) define transitions as being about a change in self-identity born out of uncertainty in the social and cultural worlds of the individual. They suggest that transitions can be best understood by taking into account the social and cultural situatedness of human thought and action. It is important to understand from this that transitions are complex and multifaceted and often involve a change in the very personality of the person involved. This might be enhanced by a period of personal reflection, development and growth by the individual student and will be different in each case.

Vygotsky (1978) developed sociocultural theory based on the premise that children develop by reconstructing cultural knowledge from previous generations of the communities into which they are born. This shows that a child's development is not just a maturing process as it exists within a historic and cultural bias and that it is profoundly influenced by the communities in which the children live. It is likely, then, that although your students will live in relative proximity to your organisation they will have come from different schools, different communities and have different personal histories. They will be undertaking different journeys and will bring different identities, beliefs and knowledge with them. The changes that take place for each student may take the form of knowledge construction, a change in identity or a change in social position, or any combination of these.

In Post-Compulsory Education and Training (PCET) the lateral transition that occurs when students move from school to college or from college to university has been researched extensively. There is a lot of research to suggest that prior experiences of learning are used to inform expectations about and comparisons with further study. The transition from one learning environment to another involves the student reflecting on their experiences of prior contexts and reconstructing this experience to adapt it to the new context. Beach (1999) identifies this transition as a struggle that has the potential to alter one's sense of self.

The difficulty arises when a student's previous experiences of education have not been positive and they bring with them baggage that impedes their ability to learn and to benefit from the experiences at the new organisation. A previously negative self-image as a student that has been reinforced throughout secondary education can be difficult to shake off and even though the new organisation offers a clean slate or new start, students can often struggle to make the most of this opportunity. We will attempt to look at strategies you could use to help students to review and reassess their self-image in chapter 2.

The uncertainty that sometimes arises from change has been referred to by Zittoun (2006) as a 'rupture'. Ruptures would not be simple everyday changes, but rather they are episodes that engender uncertainty or disquiet. As such, they need to be considered important and managed appropriately. An example of a rupture might be encountering and getting to know new people. This might involve a reorientation of identity based on how the individual is reflected through their interactions with these new people. Students go through a period of social comparison when adjusting to a new environment, comparing themselves with other students and using this comparison to see where they 'fit in'. They may situate themselves in the new group in a different social position than in previous educational experiences, intentionally or unintentionally. They may move from being a victim of bullying to a bully or vice versa. They might move from being a 'geek' to being a rebel etc. These changes might be conscious or unconscious decisions by that specific student or they might be a reflection of the make-up of the new group and the new group's pressure to conform. These transitional behaviours will be considered in more depth in chapter 4.

Wenger (1998) presents 'Communities of Practice' (CoP) as a social theory of learning where social participation in a community is central for learning to take place. No one learns in a vacuum. We all need to interact with our surroundings in order to learn and develop and Wenger identifies this social 'situatedness' as a CoP. The participation in a CoP therefore 'shapes not only what we do, but also who we are and how we interpret what we do' (Wenger 1998: 4). Transition in a CoP framework, therefore, refers to the process of joining and becoming members of a new CoP, and the transition happens not only to the individual, but also to the community itself by the very inclusion of new members. In this way transitions are very much seen as a two-way process that changes the student and also the learning organisation.

Transitions are not to be seen as isolated ventures but as a prolonged period of social interaction and active participation with others during the introduction to and the settling into new CoP. This might be over a period of weeks or months depending on the specific student. Students can be supported through this period of transition by buddies or peer supporters and also by mentors and teaching staff in both the transition organisations. We will explore these relationships further in chapter 3.

Positive peer relationships are seen to be crucial alongside the role of previous sociocultural experiences, meaning that all students will experience transitions differently. The very journey of transition is important as it is identity-shaping and students will need to be allowed to make their own meaning from the transition journey and to reflect on their personal experiences and feelings in order to re-form their own identities.

Hernandez-Martinez *et al.* (2011) suggest that there are three main areas of concern facing students during transition periods. These are:

1 The social dimension – this involves students becoming comfortable in the new organisation and making friends and acquiring a sense of belonging.
2 The continuation of curriculum and pedagogy/andragogy – this involves an awareness of the gap between educational practices in both institutions and a sustained focus by staff on how that gap can be bridged and students supported in understanding any changes.
3 Individual progression – this involves the new organisation taking into account the individual history and background of each student.

These areas will be explored in more detail in subsequent chapters. There are some very specific areas of concern about the transition into PCET from school which focus on the fact that GCSE courses do not always prepare individuals to be independent students and specifically do not prepare them for advanced level study. This will also be explored further.

Holland *et al.* (1998) discuss the concept of 'positioning' to explain how students' identities are developed through continuous participation in social organisations. This means that students are constructing themselves through their interaction with specific organisations, the programmes they study and the activities of learning. It is through this concept that we realise students construct their identities as they travel from school to college and from college to work or university, where they encounter different social relationships and are positioned in different ways in the different organisations.

Because subject studies in PCET are voluntary and selected by the students, then the identity that the student develops is often based around that subject and the career trajectory they wish to follow. This will influence their choices of subjects and further study and also their developing sense of self.

Going to college is often a major change in the social scene, and involves radical changes in curriculum, classroom practice and pedagogy/andragogy. Teachers talk differently and students are expected to be more autonomous and independent. Students who are making this transition often view it as growing up and so as a 'consequential transition' (Beach 2003) and therefore accept the intellectual changes and challenges it involves.

Beach further posits that, as a construct in education, transition refers to the appearance of a person carrying the product of learning from one task, problem, situation or institution to another. We therefore need to develop an understanding about how we experience continuity and transformation in becoming someone or something new, and how these consequential transitions influence our lives. At its core the concept of consequential transition involves a developmental change in the relation between an individual and one or more social activities. A change in relation can occur through a change in the individual, the activity or both.

Transitions are consequential when they are consciously reflected upon, struggled with and the eventual outcome changes one's sense of self and social positioning (Beach 1999).

Beach identifies four primary types of consequential transitions:

1. Lateral – lateral transitions occur when individuals move between two related activities in a single direction, e.g. school to college. Participation in one activity precedes and is replaced by participation in another activity.
2. Collateral – collateral transitions involve an individual's relatively simultaneous participation in two or more historically related activities e.g. carrying out part-time work while at college.
3. Encompassing – encompassing transitions occur within the boundaries of a social activity that is itself changing e.g. a newly-qualified teacher in their first post adapting to the policies and processes of that organisation.
4. Mediational – mediational transitions occur within educational activities that project or simulate involvement in an activity yet to be fully experienced e.g. a micro teach done as part of teacher training before professional practice is undertaken.

(Beach 1999: 114)

These four different types of consequential transitions can be experienced simultaneously or in a linear way, but each is slightly different. Students experiencing all will need help and support in order to emerge from the transition a better, more rounded person, more able to cope with the next stage of transformation in their lives. Poorly managed educational transitions often lead to students failing or dropping out of education. No one wants to see this as it often takes a long time for them to return, and their life chances are much reduced by this negative experience of education.

Martinez (2001) noted the reasons that students drop out of education fell into three categories: college, work and personal and family-related issues. There was also the suggestion that students who withdrew or dropped out had found it difficult to make friends, applied late or were less satisfied with their courses and the teaching. A key factor identified in the retention of students was strong tutor support and a strong emphasis on students getting to know each other during induction (Trotter 2004).

Mallinson (2009) conducted research with young people in danger of dropping out of education and focused on their views of preparation for transition, support and dropping out. Conclusions were drawn that the sharing of good information was vital to provide an appropriate course match, ensuring adequate support is given to students at risk of dropping out, utilising the partnerships between schools and colleges and the importance of attitudes.

The attitudes of staff and other students were identified as a crucial aspect that might cause young people to drop out. Of particular concern was how the teachers treated them and the impact of this on their self-esteem, learning and progress. Students in this study expressed their desire to be listened to and heard and also to have opportunities for fun and relaxation. They also identified a need for the curriculum to include life skills and for more differentiation to allow them to learn at their own pace, whilst being challenged and supported.

Mallinson concludes that building resilience is important and highlights the importance of students feeling confident and connected. A secure base, self-esteem, a sense of purpose and of a positive educational experience are essential. We can see from this study, and others, that it is often the 'softer' emotional side of education that makes the difference between students experiencing a smooth transition from one organisation to another. As teachers we need to acknowledge this and think clearly about how we will address these issues with our students.

Questions for you to ponder are:

1 How will you organise your induction period to ensure all students make friends and feel secure in the new organisation?
2 How will you develop students' resilience and confidence?
3 How will you develop your students as autonomous, independent students?
4 How will you develop partnerships with your feeder schools/colleges to ensure smooth transitions for your students?
5 How will you develop life skills and coping skills for your students?

Throughout the first part of this book we aim to address these issues and focus on the emotional and social aspects of transitions. Part 2 is more concerned with the pedagogical/andragogical issues involved in transitions. We strongly believe that both aspects of study are vital to a successful transition programme, but have intentionally put the emotional aspects first as, for younger students particularly, these appear to be the issues most likely to put them off education and make them drop out.

'The 14–19 education phase has been described as a period of transition – from youth to adulthood, from compulsory schooling to employment for some, from compulsory schooling into post-compulsory education and training for others' (*Nuffield Review* 2005). Whatever changes are made to the curriculum, funding or providers of 14–19 year old education, there will always be a need for staff in schools and colleges, and training providers, to deliver high quality education and training to meet the needs of these very complex students and to support them through the transition from school to college or other provision and then from there to work/university.

Mezirow developed the theory of transformational learning in the 1970s. Transformational learning claims that when individuals engage in critical reflection they reach deeper understandings of their own personal experiences and are able to use this deeper understanding to develop new perspectives on education and to re-engage with education on a different level. Mezirow states that 'Transformations may be epochal – sudden major reorientations in habit of mind, often associates with significant life crises – or cumulative, a progressive sequence of insights resulting in changes of point of view and leading to transformation in habit of mind' (Mezirow 2009: 94).

This concept of transformational learning is fundamental to understanding students and where they are placed in their own learning journeys. Some students will have undergone some form of transformation and will have a readiness to learn and some students will not yet have undertaken the self-reflection necessary to transform their own view of learning and may definitely not have a readiness to learn. This is particularly evident when the course of study being undertaken is not embarked upon willingly. Transitions are periods of change in our lives that seem to alternate with periods of stability. Transitional periods are inevitable in the lives of all people and can lead to a questioning of the formerly stable, solid foundations of a person's life. Wolf talks about Levinson's 1996 model in her book on Adulthood:

> For an individual's way of being in the world to be maintained, it must be structured. Structures are necessarily psychological structures, shaped by both biological and psychological needs as well as by social expectations. Facing the tensions involved when an existing structure seems to be working less well, and facing the need for a new structure is likely to command much of an individual's attention on repeated occasions during their life-spans.
>
> (Wolf 2005: 127)

We need to link participation to the quality of the experience. Participating on its own is not sufficient to empower and enable students to achieve. They must be able to enjoy the experience and gain emotional and academic benefits from it. Learning should involve the student as a whole person; at an emotional and personal as well as at an intellectual level; learning should be pleasurable and relevant. Rogers (2002) clearly links these issues and talks about the student as a whole person and meeting their need for a pleasurable learning experience. It is the offering of opportunities to participate and the provision of the resources and materials to support the students in that participation that will address the negative experiences of disadvantaged individuals and communities. Learning is done by individuals; each student learns in a particular way. Inclusive teaching is about helping all students to optimise their own individual learning (Race 2005).

Encouraging students to actively engage in their learning and to enjoy the experience is part of the role of the teacher. Yet the responsibility and decision to engage and enjoy the learning is that of the student. To that end, the point they are at in their learning journey and transformation must influence their receptiveness to the process of learning.

One aspect it is important to discuss before moving into the detail of how to support transitions for our students is the transitions, professionalism and professional identity of you, the staff involved in PCET settings. You are fundamental to the transition process and so this is an area worthy of consideration.

Teacher transitions, professionalism and identity

Much has been written about professionalism and our image of us as professionals within educational settings, and although much of this body of writing is about teachers in a school setting we can extrapolate from this and apply it to lecturers and managers in colleges and universities, or other educational settings.

Traditionally the term 'professional' has been synonymous with the status of doctors, lawyers and clergymen and holds within its meaning an implication that it involves some sort of 'oath' to serve the common good. Society deems that a profession such as this should be self-regulating and responsible for upholding its own ethical values, practices and behaviours via its own professional code of conduct.

One aspect of a professional group's exclusivity is cognitive exclusivity and one important method of achieving closure is credentialism – that is, having the credentials required to do the job. Such groups certify their members in terms of the knowledge they have acquired, and alongside this they try to ensure that this knowledge is difficult to obtain and maintain. This could certainly apply to teachers and lecturers as there is a prerequisite for 'knowledge expertise' within the teacher/lecturer's specialist subject. There is also the 'pedagogical/andragogical expertise' within the role of the teacher that is certified before Qualified Teacher Status (QTS) or Qualified Teacher Learning and Skills (QTLS) is 'awarded'.

The word 'profession' is a collective symbol that represents a system of ideas and beliefs about a certain job or role. The term 'profession' is widely contested (Robson 2006; Dingwall and Mcintosh 1978). The traditional concept of an occupation that has fixed defining characteristics is simplistic and lacks credibility. It is better to consider the notion of professionalism as discourse. A discourse is an inter-related set of texts and statements that constructs an object and brings it into being, discourses are not static and many can be drawn on simultaneously (Foucault 1972). Thus, in this context, professionalism is recognised as a constructive and regulatory discourse, a cultural and social practice for organising individuals and institutions (Seddon 1997; cited in Robson 2006). Foucault supports this view by positing that professional behaviours are culturally produced, to the degree that they exert a discipline and represent a form of oppression (Belsey 2002).

Reflecting on Goffman's ideas that each person has a number of 'selves', each one focusing on the execution of one role at any given time, and the fact that each person has the ability to adapt the self in order to be effective within each situation (Goffman 1959; cited in Day et al. 2006), there is often a reluctance to face such changes, perhaps because we find comfort in doing each role well, being unprepared for the transition to new challenging roles that is fundamental in education in the current climate.

Each person will have a perception of their own 'professional selves' that will not necessarily be the 'self' that others see or experience. Lacan (2006) introduces what he calls the mirror phase to fill in an apparent gap in Freud's analysis of how the ego is formed. This is explained as a process akin to a young child looking in the mirror and saying 'This is me'. The child then orientates future experiences around that original sense of self. However, that sense of self is constantly developing and the image in the mirror is never the same (Brown 2008). Lacan goes on to say that humans are the only animals capable of self-deception, illusion and disillusion (Britzman 2009) and so we are able to see ourselves in the mirror as something that is not factually accurate but is illusionary and based on our own perceptions of our selves. Using this analogy we can explore the image of ourselves that we as 'professionals' have.

Day *et al.* (2005) focus on the nature of and influences on teacher identities, both personal and professional, the multiple 'I' agency; that is, the many selves that teachers have, and their view of fragmented selves. Links are made between self-awareness and the perceived opinions of others, which Lacan (2006) likened to looking in the mirror. These theories draw upon how the 'self' is influenced by social interactions and created through language and social experiences. Day *et al.* (2005) also introduce more thought to the argument by taking into account the fact that people's lives are multifaceted. This was posited first by Goffman (1959), who presented the idea that each person has a number of 'selves', each one focusing on the execution of one role at any given time and situation. He believed the ability to adapt the self is essential in order to be effective within each situation (cited in Day *et al.* 2006).

Cooper and Olson (1996) go beyond this by identifying 'multiple selves' that are continually reconstructed through historical, cultural, sociological and psychological influences (cited in Day *et al.* 2006). This is particularly true for lecturers in this sector, as they fulfil many roles and as such reflect many 'selves'.

Ball (1972) separates the situated from the substantive identity. The situated self is a malleable presentation that differs in different situations and the substantive self is the stable core self that is fundamental to how a person thinks about themselves. Incorporating the identity of 'manager' or 'teacher' or any other 'self' into an individual's self-image is accomplished over time (Day *et al.* 2005).

Nias (1989: 193) concluded that 'teachers' inevitable inability to fully satisfy their own consciences and their wider audiences leaves them feeling simultaneously under pressure, guilty and inadequate'. MacLure (1993) espouses that identity is not a stable entity that people possess but rather is constructed within social relations. Teacher agency is also important and within hierarchical structures agency is still exercised as teachers find room to manoeuvre. Stronach *et al.* (2002) discuss the professional as 'teacher' as a unitary construct and too much of a generalisation. They propose a different reading of the professional as being caught between an 'economy of performance' (the audit culture) and various 'ecologies of practice' (disposition and commitments). This introduces the concepts of power and hierarchy to the discussion.

Dual professionalism or even multi-professionalism is a key feature of PCET as all staff have subject expertise/professionalism alongside teacher expertise/professionalism and often alongside manager expertise/professionalism. However, recent changes in government policy would seem to suggest that this dual professionalism that has been a core feature of the role for many years may be somewhat negated by the de-professionalisation of the sector. It is no longer compulsory for PCET teachers to gain a full teaching award but only to complete the initial preparatory award. As a result of the Lingfield review (2012), the only commitment to study is 'a duty placed on lecturers to continuously extend and update both their occupational and their pedagogical expertise, including through undertaking the new Cert PCET or Dip PCET where appropriate' (Lingfield 2012: 25). The question for us is will the lack of teacher qualifications affect staff's teacher professionalism? Is there an impact on identity or professionalism for staff not given the opportunity to gain either QTS or QTLS?

These areas will be explored further in subsequent chapters. Suffice to say the behaviours, identity and professionalism of staff who are involved in managing student transitions are likely to have an impact on the experience of students during these transition periods.

Transitions-focused approaches to 14–19 education

Table 1.1 outlines our proposed approach to identifying a new view of teaching 14–19 year olds. We have notionally called this a transitions-focused approach as we feel it is situated between traditional pedagogical and andragogical approaches. As such it is in itself a blurred/merged version of both existing theories. A lot of teaching in PCET in the current climate is situated in this middle ground and there is no longer a clear distinction between pedagogy – the art and science of teaching children – and andragogy – the art and science of teaching adults. Most teachers will agree that they have met 5 year olds who are andragogical students and 45 year olds who are pedagogical students.

Our aim is merely to situate our model between the two and to ensure that its major focus is on the emotional and social support of students in their journey to becoming independent and of autonomous students who can progress to university or work as active and valuable citizens able to make a real difference in society.

A transitions-focused approach could also be described as a person-centred approach. That is, we are conscious of the fact that all students will experience transitions differently and that the most important thing we can do for them as teachers is to support them during these transitions. This means we must acknowledge the fact that we must focus on each individual student.

Our two main focus areas are transition to college at either 14 or 16 years old and the transition from college to university at 18+ years old. These two areas have a lot of commonality but also some unique transitional aspects. For the most part we will talk about transitions applicable to both of these phases, but where it is appropriate to split them we will look at each separately and focus on the unique aspects of that particular transition.

It is also important to note that people can experience a lot of these transitional experiences at different ages from those we have identified. For example, adult students transitioning from college to university may experience similar emotions and behaviours as those transitioning at 18 years old. However, for ease of reference in this book we identify the two transition periods and the traditional ages at which students go through these transitions whilst acknowledging the wide variety in students and in the experiences of students in this sector. It is also important to acknowledge that we use the term college to represent sixth forms, PCET colleges, specialist colleges, training providers, work-based training and any other provider of post-compulsory education and training.

Throughout this book we will focus on the transitions experienced by our students, but we must also recognise the transitions we go through ourselves from trainee teacher to teacher, professional, manager, expert etc. Throughout our professional and personal lives we will experience transitions and we will constantly have to reflect on our journeys and re-position ourselves with the communities of practice

Table 1.1 Proposed approach

Section	Chapter	Existing pedagogical approaches and assumptions about students	Transitions-focused approaches that critically examine the needs of students	Existing andragogical approaches and assumptions about students
1 Relationships	1 Introduction – New approaches to transition phases	Students are dependent on others for educational ideas	**Students are developing capacity to explore issues and ideas**	Students have an ability to identify and think about educational issues for themselves
	2 Managing expectations	Students have a narrow understanding of personal problems and social issues	**Students need supported development of social/personal interaction and are developing an awareness of the needs of others**	Students have an altruistic concern for the welfare of others
	3 Culture, ethos and identity	Students demonstrate a readiness to learn that is dependent on the teacher	**Students' readiness to learn needs to be nurtured and encouraged**	Students bring life experiences to the learning experience and this drives their readiness to learn
	4 Managing transitional behaviour	Students display a passive acceptance of educational instruction and authority	**Students challenge existing instruction and authority and seek understanding and relevance of rules and regulations before conforming**	Students adopt an individually constructed acceptance and conformity to instruction and authority
	5 Developing independence and motivating learning using a coaching and mentoring approach	Students are motivated extrinsically by external rewards and punishment	**Students are developing a natural curiosity for learning that is slowly moving away from extrinsically determined factors**	Students are motivated intrinsically by internal incentives and natural curiosity

2 Teaching, learning and assessment

6 The planning cycle	Planning is done primarily by teachers with little or no input from students	**The needs and interests of students must be considered and used by the teacher to inform planning**	Planning is negotiated between the student and the teacher
7 The role of the teacher in supporting transitions	Teaching is didactic and prescriptive	**Teaching is creative and incorporates some self-directed learning**	Teaching is inductive and interactive
8 Ensuring a learning culture	Learning is passive and reliant upon the teacher's input	**Lessons are scaffolded and carefully facilitated to develop independent learning**	Learning is experiential and enquiry based
9 Integrating assessment for learning into the 14–19 classroom	Assessment is teacher/curriculum driven	**Assessment introduces concepts of peer and self-assessment**	Assessment is driven by student-collected evidence and validated by peers, facilitators or experts
10 Final thoughts	A final look at supporting transitions at 14/16 and consideration of preparing students for transitions at 18/19		

to which we belong. Sometimes this will involve joining new communities and always changing and adapting our identities and image of ourselves. We will constantly be faced with challenges and change and we will have to manage our own consequential transitions, hopefully with the help and support of other professionals and our families, but always with self-awareness and perception of the effect of those transitions on our students, families and colleagues and the organisation we work for.

Chapter 2

Managing expectations

Introduction

In recent years the 14–19 sector has been inundated with interventions and policy changes aimed at improving the quality of education for those engaging with the sector. A strong focus over the last few years has been on vocational education for 14–19 year olds within schools, colleges and the new academies and University Technical Colleges (UTCs). Traditionally schools have taught up to the age of 16 in compulsory education, while colleges and sixth form colleges have taught from the age of 16 in post-compulsory education. However, there has always been a crossover between the two. Fourteen has always been a crucial time in the development of young people. This can be seen throughout history, from the 1917 Lewis report that made it compulsory to stay on at school until the age of 14 to the 2009 Nuffield report that proposed fundamental changes to the education of 14–19 year olds.

For those young people who are unlikely to achieve 5 A*–C grades at GCSE, vocational provision has often been offered in the past at local colleges to prepare them for work. These 14–16 year olds who have attended colleges in the past twenty years have often been seen as difficult to reach and in danger of dropping out of education altogether. The schools have sent them to the colleges to keep them interested and they have traditionally done courses in areas such as construction, catering and hair and beauty. Staff that have been given these groups to teach have received no special training and have often struggled to maintain behaviour and achievement. Unsurprisingly this has led to disappointing results and a poor reputation for vocational options for 14 year olds.

The 14–19 phase has been described as a period of transition – 'from youth to adulthood, from compulsory schooling to employment for some, from compulsory schooling into post-compulsory education and training for others' (*Nuffield Review* 2005: 9). Whatever changes are made to the curriculum, funding or providers of 14–19 year old education, there will always be a need for staff in schools and colleges, and training providers to deliver high quality education and training to meet the needs of these very complex students and to support them through the transition from school to college or other provision and then from there to work/university.

There are many examples of different types of education for 14–19 year olds; two of these based on my own experience are given as examples here: UTCs and Steiner–Waldorf Education.

University Technical Colleges

UTCs are a new concept in education. They offer 14–19 year olds the opportunity to take a highly regarded, full-time, technically oriented course of study. They are equipped to the highest standard, sponsored by a university and offer clear progression routes at the age of 14 into Higher Education or further learning in work. The students learn in a very practical way, integrating national curriculum requirements with the technical and vocational elements. The UTC ethos and curriculum is heavily influenced by local and national employers who also provide support and work experience for students. A fundamental principle of UTCs is that they do not judge students on their past performance. Students are given new opportunities and new ways of learning that allow them to achieve to a higher level than they may have done before. We will discuss these further in chapter 8.

Steiner–Waldorf Education

Steiner-Waldorf schools are a worldwide alternative approach to the education of children and adolescents for an increasing number of families. Rudolf Steiner was an Austrian philosopher who was asked to set up a school for the children of employees at the Waldorf–Astoria factory in Stuttgart in 1919.

His approach to education is called Anthroposophy and in essence is designed to help young people develop into free, moral and integrated individuals and enable each to achieve their unique potential. As of 2010, there were 995 Steiner–Waldorf schools throughout the world. A key aspect of the education is using creative methods including art, crafts, and games and so on, to help children to learn, alongside more traditional methods.

Steiner sees adolescence as a crucial stage in development and believes that it is one of the worst times in life to concentrate wholly on oneself. Many have described adolescence as painful and, as with many things, the pain increases the more we concentrate on it. According to Steiner, the key to educating young people is therefore to teach them to shift their focus outwards onto the world outside. This necessitates teachers who have a passion, imagination and real depth of understanding for their subjects in order to encourage an open, questioning and enthusiastic response from their students.

One of Steiner's key tenets was that when educating adolescents there must be a fundamentally moral approach to the education. He felt it was very important that teachers look to themselves and their own personalities and attitudes lest they be passed on to their pupils. He was very clear that tutors/practitioners should continually develop themselves so that any of their inadequacies were not passed on to their students.

Perhaps Rudolf Steiner's approach of uncovering the core of an individual enables them to emerge as free, moral and balanced individuals who feel strong enough to deal with whatever may be thrown at them in an increasingly complex and uncertain world.

When it comes to adolescents, the overall thinking is to awaken within each young person an extraordinarily great interest in the world outside of themselves. When they are educated they must be led to look out at everything – the world, its laws, its causes and effects, into human beings and their goals but also into music and art. In Steiner's own words:

> We shouldn't ask: what does a person need to know or be able to do in order to fit into an existing social order? Rather we should ask: what lives in each person and what can be developed in him or her? Only then will it be possible to direct the new qualities of each emerging generation into society. Society will then become what young people, as whole human beings, make out of the existing social conditions. Our highest endeavour must be to develop free human beings who are able to impart purpose and direction to their lives.
>
> Rudolf Steiner

Regardless of the type of education, be it in a college, school, UTC, Studio School, Steiner school or any of the many other types of provision that exist at the moment, as a teacher educator and an experienced teacher in the PCET sector I have become increasingly aware of the difficulties students experience during these transitions phases and the need to clearly manage their expectations and experiences, particularly during the transition into new groups of students in new classrooms.

Most 14–19 year olds in education are going through a transition period in their lives, particularly those undertaking vocational training and preparing to enter a specific career. This transition period can be very challenging and can cause a negative reaction to those providing the teaching. On the other hand there can be an embracing of the new learning and opportunities opening up. This depends on the nature of the transition and the extent of the student's choice in that transitional process. It also depends on the way the transition is supported and particularly on the quality of the induction period.

Students who are 14–19 years old may already have certain well-developed ideas about life in line with their own systems and beliefs. To admit that they need to learn something new is to admit there is something incomplete with their present knowledge base. Many of these students, though they may perceive that they do need new skills or knowledge, feel so threatened by the challenge to their previous beliefs that they are unable to learn (Rogers 2007). One of our roles is to be aware of this and to ensure we encourage discussion and reflection on their motivations and barriers to learning.

Transitions are periods of change in our lives that seem to alternate with periods of stability. Transitional periods are inevitable in the lives of all young people and can lead to a questioning of the formerly stable, solid foundations of a person's life. This can be very challenging to deal with and not just for the young person but often also for their family and friends.

We need to link participation to the quality of the experience. Participating on its own is not sufficient to empower and enable students to achieve. They must be able to enjoy the experience and gain emotional and academic benefits from it.

'Learning should involve the student as a whole person; at an emotional and personal as well as at an intellectual level; learning should be pleasurable and relevant' (Rogers 1983: 6). This is much easier said than done but should be central to all of our planning and to all of our relationships in a classroom.

Encouraging students to engage actively in their learning and to enjoy the experience is part of the role of the teacher. Yet the responsibility and decision to engage and enjoy the learning is that of the students. To that end, the point they are at in their learning journey and transformation must influence their receptiveness to the process of learning.

Induction

Research clearly shows the importance of a really good induction period for students. This induction period should take place in every new learning context – so either a new course, classroom or programme. This is equally important for the move from school to college as it is for the move from college to university or work.

Induction is the most important tool in managing transitions, but also in retention of students and in creating a learning culture (see chapter 3 for more on culture, ethos and identity). Great care should be taken with the planning of the induction period and a suitable amount of time and resources should be given over to ensuring it is successful.

Many people think induction is all about showing students how to use the library and how to log on to the computers, but it is much more than that. The most important aspect of induction is that of facilitating the making of friends. Hundreds of young people drop out of education in the first couple of weeks and the most commonly stated reason they give for dropping out is not fitting in, or not making friends.

On our programmes we consider the induction period to be so important that it is always planned and delivered by me and the head of area. This shows the students how important it is but also makes it clear that we are accessible and available for students throughout their programme. Our main aim is to ensure that by the first coffee break everyone knows the names of at least two other students and by the end of the induction week they have worked with everyone in the group at least once. This ensures that everyone makes friends and never has to face having to come into a classroom and not have anyone to sit next to or talk to. We do many 'getting to know you' activities and team building exercises to build a positive group ethos from the very beginning.

The other very important part of the induction process is to share expectations, manage hopes and fears and to set ground rules for the future. Sharing expectations right at the beginning can avoid students having unrealistic expectations and is a way of opening the dialogue about rules and regulations.

Below is an example from our teacher training programme of our expectations:

What you can expect from the staff . . .

1 Professional behaviour
2 Prompt responses (within 2 working days)
3 Outstanding teaching
4 Modelling of best practice
5 Supportive Personal Tutor

6 Supportive Subject-Specific Mentor
7 Outstanding feedback on observations
8 Detailed feedback on assessments within 4 weeks
9 Research informed practice
10 Support, understanding and empathy.

What we can expect from you . . .

1 Professional behaviour
2 100 per cent attendance at university and placement
3 100 per cent commitment to own personal development
4 Contributions in class
5 Independent study/reading
6 Prompt responses (within 2 working days)
7 Striving to improve
8 Putting the welfare of your students first
9 To be creative, innovative and flexible
10 To be passionate.

Ground rules

In order to behave well, students need to be very clear what the ground rules are and what the consequences of breaking the rules will be. Teachers who involve students in drawing up ground rules and in signing up to those rules, and who consistently apply those consequences, should experience less disruption and bad behaviour.

Students will be aware of the rules, feel an ownership of them and will see that they are being implemented fairly. Your organisation will have a code of conduct or similar set of rules for students to follow. However, it is good practice to set your own rules for your own classroom.

For example: you may agree to allow students to listen to their iPods when they are working alone on tasks, but to put them away when working in groups or listening to you.

You may agree to talking while they are working as long as they are on task, or to enjoy five-minute chat breaks when key tasks have been completed.

Think carefully about the rules you want and make sure you allow students some room to negotiate. It goes without saying that there is no negotiation about things such as treating others with respect, not swearing and complying with health and safety regulations, but there may be room for negotiations about food and drink, clothing and talking.

You may find that each group you teach will set slightly different ground rules, but as long as they sign up to them and follow them, this is good. It does no harm to restate those rules at the beginning of lessons particularly for the first few weeks, so that no one 'gets into trouble' for forgetting the rules.

It is a good idea to get students either to make a poster or to print out a list of the rules and individually sign them and display them on the classroom walls. This allows you to use this as a visual prompt to remind students of what they have agreed to.

Many authors (Vizard 2007; Petty 2010) support the view that setting clear ground rules with students and not for students will raise expectations of good behaviour and will allow them to buy into the process and feel valued and secure in the classroom.

In some cases the students become self-policing, quickly identifying when others in the group are 'breaking' a rule and challenging them. This allows you to manage the learning environment in a less controlling way.

CASE STUDY 2.1: MARK HUGHES – WEST LANCASHIRE COLLEGE

In our college, we have an induction week programme that is specifically designed to get students out of their comfort zone as soon as possible, as well as become more comfortable with their peers and with their surroundings. All students are informed about where to meet at enrolment.

The students will meet in a lecture theatre and have a talk with the principal of the college, who will outline our college ethos and various different ground rules. Then the cohort will be divided into groups to undertake various activities. Each teacher is given an activity to do, and will do this activity with each group of students. The students will then meet the majority of their teachers this way, thus familiarising the students with what the staff are like and how their lessons will be delivered.

Many students, when they first start in a new educational institution, can experience nervousness due to the fear of the unknown – they are unsure about what the staff and other students will be like and, in particular across the age group I teach, will be concerned about the possibility that they will not make any friends in their peer group. The activities themselves are designed to enable the students to get to know their peers and the staff and immediately make friends, so that they feel less nervous and unconfident. Ultimately, this will result in happier students who will be more enthusiastic when the subjects actually start in the next week of college.

One activity that I have found to be particularly successful in these lessons is a 'time capsule' activity. It is fairly simple and only requires coloured pens and paper – I will put the students into pairs and then get the students to draw small pictures to represent their likes and dislikes. The other student in the pair has to guess what the first student is trying to represent with their picture. Then, the pictures will be locked away in their tutor files and shown again to them in their last tutorial lesson of the year. This part of the activity is often a source of amazement to the students because they are surprised at how much their tastes have changed over that period of time, and some of them even recognise how much they have 'grown up' as well.

In between these activities we also have tours that take each group across campus and show them where the library is and what it can do for each student – particularly when coursework is due or they need to do some last-minute cramming before an exam, as well as where their classrooms are for each subject. Also, each student will be shown the sports hall and where other enrichment activities take place.

Lastly, the students will have introductory lessons in each of their subjects. The A-level programme has a diverse array of subjects within it, which means that many of the students have chosen subjects that they have not encountered before, but perhaps is a passion of theirs (some even choose a subject because it sounds interesting to them upon enrolment, particularly when they need a fourth subject). This is a vital part of the process then, as the students will want to know what the newer subjects are about, as well as gauge what the subjects they are familiar with are actually like as an A-level subject. Many of them will also be curious about who their classmates will be and how well they will fit in. The introductory lessons themselves will contain the preliminary information about each subject, as well as course booklets and some more fun activities to ease the students into their new subjects and a different way of thinking.

Developing resilience

Resilience is the ability to adapt well to adversity, trauma, tragedy, threats or even significant sources of stress. One of the most difficult things for us to help young people with is their ability to develop resilience and to be able to understand and use their own emotions to help them in their learning journeys.

Building resilience can help our students manage stress and feelings of anxiety and uncertainty.

Resilience research tells us . . .

- All people have the capacity to adapt to the challenges of life when they have the support they need.
- Most young people will develop into productive adults, despite risky environments.
- Resilience is not a magical trait that a few special people have. Rather, it is 'ordinary magic' that is a part of healthy development.
- Supportive environments feature caring relationships, high expectations and opportunities for meaningful participation.

What you can do . . .

- Always build from strengths. Using activities that a student likes can get them past the things they don't.
- Schedule one-to-one time to listen to your students. It will give you incredible insights into their world.
- Many students surprise us by becoming highly successful later in life. Ensure that every student gets that chance in your class.
- Explicit 'I care' statements from teachers guarantee that students recognise the supportive environment.

Emotional intelligence

Emotional Intelligence is about being able to motivate oneself, to persist in the face of frustrations, control impulse, delay gratification and to regulate one's moods and to keep distress from swamping the ability to think, to empathise and to hope. Students need to know their own emotions, manage emotions, motivate themselves, recognise emotions in others and handle relationships. Teachers need to use their own emotional intelligence as well as helping their students to develop their own emotional intelligence. It is important to model resilience and emotional intelligence so that students can see exactly what we mean and learn from our examples.

Employability

Recently Lord Baker launched his new vision for 14–19 education, Career Colleges that will be established by PCET Colleges and will specialise in subjects offering excellent career prospects in the local labour market. These will include hospitality, catering and tourism, finance and insurance, health care, sport and event management, and construction. Each College will be supported by local employers, who will help design and deliver the curriculum. They will offer 'real-world' challenges, coupled with work experience – enabling students to develop their wider employability skills.

Career Colleges will join UTCs and Studio Schools as an alternative path to success for young people, specifically those beginning at 14. One of the common criticisms of transferring at 14 is that it narrows down options for young people, that they are required to choose a 'job for life' when they are barely a teenager. However, I wonder how many of us are in the same job, or even the same industry, we started in fresh out of college or university? Far from closing doors, being exposed to the world of work early on actually leads to many more being opened.

One of the key components of all of these new initiatives is the focus on preparing young people for employment and in developing their employability skills.

Functional skills are essential skills in English, Mathematics and ICT that enable everyone to deal with the practical problems and challenges of life. Functional skills are used in everyday situations. They help us to recognise good value deals when making a purchase, write an effective application, or use the internet to access local services or online banking.

> Functional skills will provide individuals with the essential knowledge, skills and understanding that will enable them to operate confidently, effectively and independently in life and work.
>
> 14–19 education and skills: implementation plan (DfES 2005)

Some interesting facts . . .

5 million adults in the UK cannot read the Yellow Pages
7 million cannot work out the correct amount of medicine to give a child
These adults do not have the skills to function and progress in everyday life and work.

(Francis and Gould 2009: 65)

Functional skills are offered as standalone qualifications. They are also embedded in adult programmes in four ways:

1 Discrete: taught and assessed by specialists as a separate topic from the main area of learning.
2 Partly embedded: taught by specialists and applied in a flexible way within the main programme.
3 Mostly embedded: taught by specialists with reinforcement and application through a range of purposeful contexts across the programme.
4 Fully embedded: taught, developed and applied across the learning programme by all teachers using naturally occurring opportunities for functional skills development.

Employability is a set of attributes, skills and knowledge that all labour market participants should possess to ensure that they have the capability of being effective in the workplace – to the benefit of themselves, their employer and the wider economy. There are ten top employability skills:

* self-management
* team working
* problem solving
* communication – application of literacy
* customer care/business awareness
* application of numeracy
* application of ICT
* motivation and enthusiasm
* oral communication
* flexibility and adaptability.

What you can do . . .

- Make sure you take every opportunity to embed functional skills into your lessons.
- Always link what you are covering to the wider employability agenda.
- Get employers involved as much as possible.
- Offer the opportunity for students to undertake practice interviews etc.
- Be aware of the local job market and what skills your students might need to be developing.
- Look for opportunities to enhance their wider skills, such as teamwork, problem solving etc.
- Have high expectations of your students and their employment prospects.
- Prepare them for the world of work by modelling behaviours such as good timekeeping, good manners etc.
- Develop independence and autonomy in your students.
- Help them with CV writing.
- Encourage students to take part in extra-curricular activities.
- Try to encourage work experience opportunities.
- Always be encouraging of their hopes and dreams.

Moving on in education

If students are not planning to move into employment, they are often planning to move into Further/Higher Education. They will still need help and support to make this transition as it will involve either a change in organisation or a change in the level and programme of study.

The skills needed for higher education are very similar to those needed for employment and can include:

- self-management/independence and autonomy
- team working
- communication – application of literacy
- problem solving
- application of numeracy
- application of ICT
- motivation and enthusiasm
- oral communication
- flexibility and adaptability.

Moving into Higher Education can also often mean moving away from home, so they will need the added skills of:

- managing a budget
- life skills such as cooking and washing clothes

- making friends
- dealing with being alone.

What you can do . . .

- Make sure you take every opportunity to embed functional skills into your lessons.
- Always link what you are covering to further study opportunities.
- Offer help with UCAS forms etc.
- Offer the opportunity for students to undertake practice interviews etc.
- Be aware of Higher Education and what skills your students might need to be developing.
- Look for opportunities to enhance their wider skills, such as teamwork, problem solving etc.
- Have high expectations of your students and their education prospects.
- Prepare them for the world university by modelling behaviours such as good timekeeping, good manners etc.
- Develop independence and autonomy in your students.
- Encourage students to take part in extra-curricular activities.
- Always be encouraging of their hopes and dreams.

Citizenship and education

As far back as the Greek city-states and the Roman republic, citizenship has meant involvement in public affairs by those who had the rights of citizens: to take part in public debate and in shaping the laws and decisions of a country. By the beginning of the twentieth century there was an organisation – the Moral Instruction League – whose aim was to influence the school curriculum. This was renamed after the First World War to the Civics and Moral Education League. In 1934 this became the Association for Education in Citizenship, who advocated direct training for citizenship rather than the indirect method of general education working through existing subjects.

The areas covered by citizenship have developed and broadened to include all classes of society and have widened to include freedom of the press and the opening up of the process of government.

When making citizenship part of the national curriculum the Lord Chancellor said:

> We should not, must not, dare not, be complacent about the health and the future of British democracy. Unless we become a nation of engaged citizens, our democracy is not secure.
>
> Citizenship is more than a subject. If taught well and tailored to local needs, its skills and values will enhance democratic life for all of us, both rights and responsibilities, beginning in school and radiating out.
>
> Bernard Crick, National Curriculum Citizenship, 1999

Although citizenship education is no longer compulsory, it is a vital part of young people's development and of making them ready for employment, ensuring their expectations are clear of their role as active citizens in our society. It is the role of education to help them get ready for this responsibility.

Young people should leave school or college with an understanding of the political, legal and economic functions of adult society, and with the social and moral awareness to thrive in it. Citizenship education is about enabling people to make their own decisions and to take responsibility for their own lives and their communities. It is not about trying to fit everyone into the same mould, or about creating 'model' or 'good' citizens. Schools and colleges should not simply teach citizenship but should model it in the way they run and organise themselves.

Citizenship education should include such things as . . .

- awareness of their rights and responsibilities as citizens
- information about the social and political world
- awareness of the welfare of others
- the ability to articulate in their opinions and arguments
- being capable of having an influence on the world
- being active in their communities
- being responsible in how they act as citizens.

These capacities do not develop unaided. They have to be learned. While a certain amount of citizenship may be picked up through ordinary experience in the home or at work, it can never in itself be sufficient to equip citizens for the sort of active role required of them in today's complex and diverse society.

Skills developed in young people . . .

- Develops self-confidence to successfully deal with significant life changes and challenges such as bullying and discrimination;
- Gives them a voice: in the life of their schools, in their communities and in society at large;
- Enables them to make a positive contribution by developing the expertise and experience needed to claim their rights and understand their responsibilities and preparing them for the challenges and opportunities of adult and working life.

What you can do . . .

- Be an active citizen yourself and share your experiences with your students.
- Never miss an opportunity to link your subject to the wider moral, social or political climate.
- Always discuss current issues and encourage your students to have an opinion.
- Undertake projects/fund-raising activities aimed at helping/improving your local community.
- Encourage students to take up roles as representatives of their peers within the organisation.
- Make sure your students understand about their right to vote and encourage them to use it.
- Link citizenship to employability and to everyday life.

Chapter 3

Culture, ethos and identity

Introduction

> I have come to a frightening conclusion: I am the decisive element in the classroom. It is my personal approach that creates the climate. It is my daily mood that makes the weather. As a teacher I possess tremendous power to make a young person's life miserable or joyous. I can be a tool of torture or an instrument of inspiration. I can humiliate or humour, hurt or heal. In all situations it is my response that decides whether a crisis will be escalated or de-escalated, a young person humanised or de-humanised.
>
> (Ginott 1972: 5)

The culture and ethos of an organisation and the identity of the students within that organisation are really important; we can create a culture and ethos that is supportive and caring or we can create one that is uncaring and bullying or anything in between. However, it is not down to an individual to create that ethos and culture, it is the whole organisation and its collective behaviours that create the culture and ethos. We can, however, contribute to this culture and ethos in a positive way and we can certainly control the culture and the ethos within our own classrooms. This chapter will look at the role of culture and ethos in supporting transitions and in helping students to find their own identities within the new setting. However, this culture and ethos come out of the collective behaviours of the organisation and, as such, it is important to look at the role of managerialism, accountability, risk and change in order to then get to an understanding of how culture is developed in education organisations.

Managerialism, accountability, risk and change

The questioning of professionals' rights and freedoms has been rooted in a deeper questioning of the professionals' claim to extraordinary knowledge in the matter of human importance (Schon 1991), and this has led to more 'managerialism' and accountability for the professions.

There is evidence that over recent decades PCET has gradually been appropriated by managerialist ideology often originating outside of the sector. Since the 1980s this increasingly directive and prescriptive regime, which began with the requirement to document course content through to teaching observations and the requirement for academics to document their time, has led to academics functioning within performative systems of accountability embedded in managerialism. This managerialism rejects the primacy of the professional, and imposes a range of subjectives that encourage individuals to behave in the best interests of the organisation. For academics this implies less freedom and autonomy and a more structured, monitored and managed regime than in the past (Kolsaker 2008).

The PCET discourse has been altered and programmatised through centrally funded programmes of 'innovation'. The very nature of centrally funding and monitoring 'innovation' means that innovation in this discourse applies to ideas for change that are consistent with institutional, and, in turn, national priorities. Findlow (2008) discusses such programmatisation, identifying that such programmes require academic innovators who seek funding to adopt the language and procedures of a management/audit culture, whose driving values are efficiency, transparency and standardisation. These managerial discourses are not necessarily aligned to academic discourses. She goes on to say that accountability is intrinsic to academia, but qualifies it by defining this accountability as that which is about honesty and responsibility, about making decisions based on sound rationales and on the understanding that one might be called to account at any point. Strathern (2000) supports this by suggesting that audit is almost impossible to criticise in principle as it advances values that academics hold dear, such as responsibility and openness about outcomes. The move towards a 'harder' accountability in the sector has led to the environment, both nationally and institutionally, demanding subscription to a view of accountability that impedes innovation, risk taking and change and is based on an absence of trust.

The current climate is also responsible for the almost constant need to change: change to meet government directives, national priorities and pressures and to remain viable institutions. The need to navigate and implement change and adapt to it is widespread. Hanna (2003) points to the challenges of leading within the uncertain environment, which involves having the courage to take action when the longer term way ahead remains unclear. Kotter (2007) sees the ability to guide change as the ultimate test of a leader. Scott *et al.* (2008: 27) talk of the need to assist academic leaders in 'making sense of the continuously and rapidly changing context' in which they operate and that overall 'what emerges is how important it is for academic leaders to be able to deal with change'. These studies and many more lead us to see that one of the major roles of the managers and teachers is that of facilitating and implementing change, especially within educational organisations.

Ramsden (1998) observes that academics fundamentally understand change, but to accept change, they need to see change and innovation as being genuinely beneficial to their work. He goes on to suggest the dissent encountered is caused often by leaders underestimating resistance and failing to pay attention to 'the need to gain shared consent within a culture that so values autonomy and cooperative decision making' (Ramsden 1998: 122).

Hanna (2003) believes it is more effective to focus on the people who are expected to embrace strategic change rather than focusing on the structure itself. This is supported by Wheatley (2003), who argues that change leadership calls for a focus on the people expected to work with the change rather than relying on a devised system or structure. A number of difficulties of managing change in colleges/universities where strong democratic and anti-managerial traditions exist are posited by Middlehurst (2007: 70); these include the problem of managing highly individualistic academics with no strong sense of corporate identity to the department or setting.

Allen (2003) found that innovation was facilitated by the confidence that comes with secure working environments. Where change was successful, it tended to emerge from environments where holistic and humanistic views of scholarship and systems of implicit trust were embedded. These gave academics the confidence to take risks. Allen also found that insecure environments created distrust and removed the expectation and obligation for genuinely responsible academic accountability and made staff reluctant to devote time, signpost problems or to try something that might not work and might reflect negatively on their careers. This institution-driven culture of risk avoidance has, Allen believes, contributed to stress, professional dissatisfaction and falling standards, as well as a reduced capacity to innovate.

It is important to keep a central understanding that you are working in an existing, hierarchical organisation and have no individual power or voice to change this. Our actions are taken as an employee of that organisation and we are at all times trying to please those higher placed in the hierarchy and to make a success of the role of the teacher.

Post-structuralist discourse suggests that what happens, and how the culture of an organisation develops, is a product of the power relations at play within education, and in particular your organisation. Your role as a teacher invests you with a perceived power over those you teach and as such removes from them any real ability to resist any imposed rules or to truly give their consent to them. The hierarchy that exists in an organisation makes it very difficult for teachers to develop a professional identity as independent professionals, as participatory, collegiate management is not possible within the structures that exist today, nor is it supported by national policy and priorities.

Culture and ethos

Culture could be described as . . .

- 'the underlying assumptions about the way work is performed; what is acceptable and not acceptable; and what behaviour and actions are encouraged and discouraged' (Atkinson 1990);
- 'it's the way we do things around here!';
- organisational 'glue';
- an integrating mechanism;
- the thing that guides and shapes behaviour.

Cultural hierarchy – Schein (1985)

Schein puts forward his cultural hierarchy that suggests that we can understand the culture of an organisation by looking at three different aspects of that organisation.

1 Artefacts – most visible level – the things that represent the culture of an organisation. A college that celebrates the success of its students visibly via posters etc. shows that it has a culture of valuing students.
2 Values – the moral and ethical working codes that guide people in uncertain situations and influence thoughts and behaviour.
3 Basic assumptions – unconsciously held learned responses and the organisational ethos.

All of these three things will allow us to interpret the culture of the organisation and, thus, decide if we want to be part of it and buy into its culture and ethos.

Deal and Kennedy (1982)

Deal and Kennedy suggest that there are various signifiers that we can look at to identify the culture of an organisation. These are:

- the shared values and beliefs;
- heroes and heroines – and the celebration of these;
- ritual – the rituals that form part of the organisation's behaviours;
- ceremony – the opportunities taken to celebrate success and to communicate with staff and students;
- stories – the stories that form part of the history of the organisation;
- informal network of cultural players – who are the key players in determining the culture?

Again, using these to measure the culture of the setting will allow you to find your way to fitting in and adopting the culture of the organisation.

Features of college/organisational culture

These features can be attributed to the culture of an organisation and can be used to identify what makes up the culture and ethos of an organisation. It

- learns from the internal and external environments
- influences the internal environment
- is partly unconscious
- is influenced by the past
- is commonly held
- is unlikely to be wholly uniform.

Functions of culture

- provides a common language
- provides criteria for inclusion and exclusion
- provides criteria for success/failure
- provides social guidelines.

The importance of culture

The importance of culture is that it helps reduce complexity and uncertainty and provides consistency in an organisation. People know what to expect so it enhances decision making and helps coordination of staff and resources. It is a key feature of control and contributes to effectiveness and success.

The following activities might help you to think about the culture of your own organisation:

1. Draw an image that sums up the culture of your organisation.
2. If your college was a car what would it be?
3. List six adjectives that describe your organisational culture.
4. If you were in a position to do so, which would you choose to change?
5. Which would you choose to celebrate?
6. What would a teacher recently appointed to your organisation say about its culture?
7. What would a teacher with 8 years' experience in the organisation say about it? Why might their view be different?
8. What might a student say?

When I think back to previous organisations I have worked in I would describe one of them as a big multi-coloured camper van in which everyone was welcome and another as a new red Porsche, fast and brash and a top performer – which of these would you send your children to? Which one would you want to work in? It is a personal choice but it is very clear to all in each organisation exactly what the culture and ethos is and what they need to do in order to be able to fit in!

Culture and leadership

In organisations, real power and energy is generated through relationships. The pattern of relationships and the capacity to form them is often seen as more important than the tasks, functions, roles and positions that people hold. Traditional leadership is based on positional authority linked to a formal hierarchy, with a range of different levels of authority and power at each level in the hierarchy.

According to Busher (2006) power is often perceived as having two main forms: that of authority arising from the office that a person holds and that of influence that comes from a person's personal and professional skills and knowledge, and also the interpersonal relationships they construct (Busher 2006).

Senior (2010) puts forward the case that power exists, to a large extent, only in the eye of the beholder, meaning it is not always the resources or knowledge controlled that give someone power but rather the belief by others that that person has the power of control. In effect people have to believe that you have the power in order to allow you to have the power. Each member of the team may perceive this in a different way and so may respond to the process in different ways.

As the goals and experiences of each individual team member are unique, so the organisation itself cannot exist as a coherent whole but will rather be a sum of the range of different perspectives and experiences of those individual participants (Lumby 2001). This means that whatever the structure on paper, the reality will be a mixture of connected beliefs and activities.

Lumby posits two overarching purposes for structure, control and coordination, and points out that there is a tension between these two, one often being achieved at the expense of the other. The trend in recent years has been to try and move away from control and towards a more distributed, coordinated approach to hierarchical structures.

In the current political climate of austerity and insecurity in the public sector there is also a particular emphasis on culture within leadership, and Ball (2008) puts forward leadership as being more about 'hearts and minds' rather than structures. He goes on to state that leadership within education is more about changing teachers and working collaboratively than a framework for developing leaders.

A move towards flexible and flatter organisations has led to increasingly fewer managers and so the issues of communication acquire a much increased importance, with a pressure exerted on managers to implement structures that facilitate communication laterally and vertically.

Power cannot be projected successfully unless those being led give their consent, whether that is derived willingly or by any form of perceived coercion. Manufactured consent is a form of coercion where those being consulted with agree with the person in a position of power because they feel this is what that person wants to hear and as such this will provide the best outcome for them in the long run.

A climate of trust, openness and the removal of barriers would be necessary in order to allow fully participatory decision making to take place. It is unlikely that this could take place within a traditionally hierarchical organisation.

What you can do . . .

- Be aware of the culture of the organisation you work in – you may not be able to change it, but you can understand it and how it affects your students.
- Think very carefully about the culture and ethos you engender in your classroom.
- Make sure you ensure there is a culture of openness and fairness by modelling these behaviours.
- Ensure you treat everyone with respect and expect your students to do the same.
- Move students around all the time so that they have to work with everyone in the group – this will avoid cliques forming and will encourage a group identity.

- Celebrate success both inside the classroom and outside – let other staff and parents/carers know when students have done well.
- Use praise to reward and motivate all students, remember to praise the good and have consequences for the bad!
- Always show that you enjoy your job and that you like the group you are teaching – let them know they are special and why you enjoy teaching them.
- Try to create a group ethos and encourage whole group activities – such as trips and visits.

Identity

Each person will have a perception of their own 'self' that will not necessarily be the 'self' that others see or experience. Lacan (2006) introduces what he calls the mirror phase to fill in an apparent gap in Freud's analysis of how the ego is formed. This is explained as a process akin to a young child looking in the mirror and saying 'this is me'. The child then orientates future experiences around that original sense of self. However, that sense of self is constantly developing and the image in the mirror is never the same (Brown 2008). Lacan goes on to say that humans are the only animals capable of self-deception, illusion and disillusion (Britzman 2009), and so we are able to see ourselves in the mirror as something that is not factually accurate but is illusionary and based on our own perceptions of ourselves.

A teacher may exhibit many 'selves' or images of their professional selves depending on their circumstances; indeed, today's professional has been described as mobilising a complex of occasional identities in response to shifting contexts (Day *et al.* 2006).

As a professional whose many selves include manager, teacher, counsellor, administrator, leader and friend, it is difficult to define the role in general but also to see how it could be maintained throughout any change process.

Students also have a myriad of 'selves' or images of themselves that also depend on their circumstances, and these 'selves' can change during transitions into new settings and will be strongly influenced by external things such as their peer group, their perceived position in the group and their relationship with the teacher. We can all remember examples of students who have been as good as gold in school and then become 'the rebel' in college or vice versa! We can all also cite examples of students who are great for us in our classes, but are a nightmare for other teachers. Students can be really good at college but rebellious at home and so on. What we really need to be aware of is that this variety of 'selves' is perfectly normal and we need to try to help them to position themselves within our groups and settings to enable them to find an identity that is positive and helps them to grow and develop into mature adults who are more confident in their identity and position in life.

Personality preferences are similar to the inclination you have for writing with your left or right hand. Writing with your preferred hand is more natural and comfortable, and it takes less energy and thought. With practice, though, you could write well with the other hand. Similarly, students are most comfortable when they can use their learning preferences. Even though they can learn to operate outside of their preferences, it takes more effort, which can hamper their learning. Without an understanding of the differences teachers tend to rate more favourably students with learning styles and personalities similar to their own. When the teachers start to understand the behaviour of students with different personalities, they can adjust the structure and flow of their classrooms to allow for success for more students.

Here are some of the personality types that you could find in your classroom and students either consciously or subconsciously become at least one of these 'selves'. This is taken from the work of Derrick Meador (2013).

Bully – bullies typically pick on students who either cannot or will not defend themselves. Bullies themselves are often exceedingly insecure people who prey on weaker individuals. There are physical, verbal and cyber bullies. Most students will not stand up for students who are being bullied for fear of repercussions. (See chapter 4 for more on bullying.)

Class Clown – every classroom has one or several students who believe it is their job to keep the remainder of the class entertained. These students love the attention and make it their primary goal to get laughs. This often gets these students into trouble and they are often subject to behaviour consequences.

Clueless – these students do not understand social cues or sarcasm. They can be easy targets for bullies, especially verbal bullying. They are often referred to as 'blonde' or 'air heads'. They are typically laid back and easy going.

Motivated – a motivated student is often an extremely hard worker with specific goals that they are trying to achieve. They may or may not be naturally smart, but they can typically overcome any learning issue through hard work. Teachers love to have motivated students because they are eager to learn, ask questions and do anything to reach their goals.

Natural Leader – the natural leader is someone whom everyone looks up to. They are typically tremendously enthusiastic, well liked, and well-rounded individuals. They often do not even realise that other people look up to them. Natural leaders often lead by example, but have the unique ability to get people to listen to them when they do speak.

Nerd/Geek – typically, nerds/geeks have above average intelligence. They are often seen as different or quirky and are physically immature for their age. This makes them targets for bullies. They have unique interests compared to their peers and are often fixated on those interests.

Organised – these students are almost always prepared for class. They seldom forget to complete homework and bring what they need to class. They are always on time and ready to learn when class begins. They do not forget deadlines and are adept at staying on task and managing their time.

Pot Stirrer – a pot stirrer loves to create drama without being in the centre of the situation. They look for little pieces of information that they can use to turn one student against another. These students are master manipulators even changing the story to ensure that there is drama. They understand what buttons to push and are excellent at doing that.

Quiet as a Mouse – these students are often shy and/or withdrawn. They only have a few friends and those friends are also typically quiet. They are never in trouble, but they rarely participate in classroom discussions. They avoid conflict and stay clear of drama. It can be extremely difficult for a teacher to gauge how well these students are learning.

Respectful – these students never have anything unpleasant to say. They are always on task and are typically well liked. They may not be the most popular students, but no one has anything unpleasant to say about them. They say please, thank you, and excuse me. They respond to people in authority well.

Smart Alec – these students are extremely sarcastic, argumentative and confrontational. They question or comment on everything that anyone including the teacher says. They are often sharp witted and are able to respond quickly to any situation. These students have a unique ability to get under a teacher's skin and enjoy doing just that if you let them!

Socialite – a socialite would always have something to say and find it difficult to go even a few minutes without talking. They love classroom discussions and are the first to raise their hands when the teacher asks a question. There is no limit to the topic. They are experts at everything and love to hear their own voice.

Unmotivated – an unmotivated student is typically labelled as lazy. They do not have the drive to succeed academically. They are just there because they have to be. In many cases, they do not have the necessary parental support at home to be successful. They frustrate teachers because many have tremendous potential, but refuse to complete assignments or care about their future outcomes.

Unorganised – these students genuinely frustrate a teacher. They continuously forget to take homework or important notes home. They often turn in crumpled work due to being crammed inside a locker, backpack, or book. They are often late to class and are terrible at managing their time.

This is not an exhaustive list, and if you add in to the classroom dynamic those students with identified learning difficulties or needs then you can clearly see why it is so hard for teachers to create a culture of learning and a positive environment for all students. I remember when I went to college I decided to reinvent myself – everyone in my class was new and no one knew me from school, so I decided to be one of the cool kids – to be 'hard' and not to allow myself to be led by others – I wanted to be a leader. So I reinvented my wardrobe and my behaviour and consciously made friends with others who were 'cool'. I did this consciously but many young people do it subconsciously – taking on the identity of the group of people that they make friends with on the first day and staying within this group. This is where the teacher has the power to influence these identities during the transition into a new classroom. You can observe and intervene and move students about to ensure the group settles down and takes on the identities that we would like them to – ensuring no one takes on the role of the bully for example and that 'geeks' make friends with socialites etc.

What you can do . . .

- Be aware of personality types and those you wish to encourage.
- Use the induction period to settle your group down and to 'manipulate' friendship groups.
- Talk to your students on a one-to-one basis to discuss their hopes and fears in relation to your classes.
- Praise positive behaviours.
- Encourage whole group work and mix up group tasks.
- Be aware that students change and they may do this during the period you are teaching them.
- Use role models to reinforce positive behaviours.
- Encourage self-reflection and growth.
- Be aware of the social and emotional learning that takes place in a classroom.

Chapter 4

Managing transitional behaviour

Introduction

> If you want to gather honey, don't kick over the beehive.

Managing transitional behaviour is one of the most important aspects of the role of the teacher because you really do have to start as you mean to go on! Get it right during the transition phase and you will find that you have few problems during the rest of your course. Ensuring that we are consistent and set clear ground rules, and that we understand how to ensure a 'behaviour for learning' approach will be discussed at length as most new teachers feel that 'managing behaviour' is the most challenging aspect of the role. During the transition from one organisation to another many students will arrive with preconceived ideas and thoughts about the new setting, will have set patterns of behaviour or will have experienced difficult or challenging events in their previous setting and may be difficult to motivate or engage with at the start. It is important to remember that every one of these students will have some talent, interest or passion and our job is to nurture this spark and develop it by providing a safe and secure environment for those students to develop and explore and, most importantly, to learn. It seems simple to say 'motivate' students and then they will learn! But how do we do that? What is motivation and how can we motivate people to learn? This chapter will explore this issue in some depth and will make specific links to how you can start this process quickly in order to smooth the transition from one environment to another. We will also discuss factors that affect motivation and our role in supporting students in developing and becoming active citizens who respect difference and treat each other with respect. This chapter is based on previous work by me and adapted and updated based on research and feedback from the trainee teachers we work with. It draws from Duckworth *et al.* (2010) and Bostock and Wood (2012).

Behaviour for learning

The 14–19 education and training sector is very diverse and is rapidly changing. There are more and more young people in education who are demotivated or disengaged and this must be reflected in how we manage behaviour. This means taking into account the need to engage 14–19 year olds and to ensure our expectations are demanding and ambitious and allow students to be stretched and challenged.

'Behaviour for learning' as opposed to 'managing behaviour' implies a shift in attitude from teachers and puts the emphasis on their shoulders to plan for good behaviour instead of expecting the worst.

'Behaviour for learning' is not a traditional theory but it is more of a movement to change the emphasis from managing bad behaviour to planning for good behaviour. This, for some teachers at least, will be a new way of thinking. It implies a key role for teachers in improving students' attitudes and in taking responsibility for their role in incidents of unsatisfactory conduct that occur in their classrooms.

There is an emphasis on the crucial link between the way in which young people learn and their social knowledge and behaviour. The focus is upon establishing positive relationships, setting clear ground rules for behaviour, being consistent in our dealings with students and praising and rewarding success.

As a result of research and personal experience we believe that behaviour for learning can be split into three components: planning, engaging students and rewarding success.

Are we apiarists?

If you deal carelessly with bees you will injure them, and will yourself be injured. And so with men.

Leo Tolstoy

In order to discuss these three components in detail I am going to use the analogy of the teacher as the 'apiarist' or 'bee-keeper'. This is an analogy that we use with trainee teachers in order to help them to understand the behaviour of students and their role in that behaviour.

Some key facts about bees

- Honey bees are not domesticated and the bee-keeper does not control the creatures.
- The bee-keeper owns the hives or boxes and associated equipment.
- The bees are free to forage or leave as they desire.
- Bees usually return to the bee-keeper's hive as the hive presents a clean, dark, sheltered abode.

As you can see this analogy works well as young people are not fully 'domesticated' in the sense that they are not always aware of the long term benefits of education and positive behaviour and the teacher does not control them but merely helps and encourages them to do what it is that they need to do in order to learn – or make the 'honey'.

The teacher is in charge of the classrooms and the learning environment and the culture of that environment, but the students do not have to stay; however, they do tend to return to the classes they enjoy and feel safe and valued in.

Young people are particularly vulnerable to peer pressure and to emotional reactions to external situations. We can often see the consequences of this in the classroom when their emotional distress manifests itself in bad or disruptive behaviour; we can liken this to when a bee stings someone – it is often as a result of fear or danger that the bee stings, it is never just for the fun of it!

If we try and remember this analogy we can think about how we as teachers occupy the role of the bee-keeper. We are the people who care for the bees, we ensure they have a safe environment and are rewarded for producing the honey. The bee-keeper wears protective clothing to avoid being stung as the teacher dons a protective mask so that it is not the person who is stung but the 'teacher' and so we are able to protect ourselves emotionally from any personal issues with the students.

Planning

Detailed planning will enable you to be proactive rather than reactive in establishing a suitable environment for learning, ensuring that the beehive is clean, safe and ready for the bees to make honey. If you do not give the impression of competence, knowledge and the ability to control and direct learning then the students will switch off very quickly and will show their frustration by behaving badly – the bees need to have confidence in the bee-keeper.

Planning lessons to avoid situations that might trigger challenging behaviour and thinking about possible triggers in advance will avoid the opportunities for behaviour to deteriorate, and also avoid being stung by the bees. However, it is also about planning for and expecting good behaviour. In order to behave well students need to be very clear what the ground rules are and what the consequences of breaking the rules will be. It is important that you involve students in drawing up ground rules and in signing up to those rules and that you consistently apply those consequences. This means you should experience less disruption and challenging behaviour as students will be aware of the rules and will see that they are being implemented fairly. The bees will feel that they can safely get on without disruptions to their routine and will consequently be more productive.

The quality of your lesson planning will have a direct effect on the behaviour in your classroom; therefore, planning and organising groups for group work activities beforehand and having this already on the desks or on the board gives students the impression that it is not negotiable and they have time to adjust to the planned activity.

Being aware of the underlying tensions and issues in a class and subtly reflecting this in the planning ensures that learning can take place and signals to the students that the lecturer is aware and listening to their concerns and adapts their planning to reflect this.

You need to reflect regularly on your experiences in the classroom and adapt your strategies accordingly. Further detail will be provided in chapter 6.

In reflecting on experiences of challenging behaviour in the classroom it is important to acknowledge the extent of your own responsibilities and the extent to which your actions have influenced the behaviour of the students. By acknowledging your own role in the incident you can devise strategies for responding differently in the future. Being perceptive to the dynamics of the class and the internal relationships that exist will help you to avoid situations where challenging behaviour can become an issue. The bee-keeper is nearly always to blame if he/she gets stung as it is often a sudden change or unexpected behaviour that has caused the bee to feel insecure and thus vulnerable resulting in the bee sting.

Engaging students

Young people experience a barrier to learning when something else occupies their minds, preventing them from focusing the necessary attention on what is to be learned. There are so many different things that can cause young people to get distracted or disengaged from learning and it is your job to manage the learning experience; but it is difficult to manage any situation unless you take accurate notice of what is happening with your students and the dynamics in the classroom.

Lessons need to be well structured and planned to engage students in the learning; activities should be interesting, varied and valuable; and the objectives for each activity should be shared with the students. Students are less likely to misbehave if they are engaged and working hard and behaviour for learning encourages you to take time and effort in the planning of interesting lessons that are enjoyable and that ensure learning is taking place.

Lecturers are also responsible for ensuring equality and fairness in the classroom.

> All students must feel that they are positively and equally valued and accepted, and that their efforts to learn are recognised, and judged without bias.
>
> (Petty 2004: 81)

The second key factor in behaviour for learning is to make sure students are always engaged in their learning and that work is neither too easy nor too difficult. Differentiation is essential to ensure that the needs of all students are planned for and work is suitable for all students. 'Differentiation is adopting strategies that ensure success in learning for all, by accommodating individual differences of any kind' (Petty 2004: 541).

Students in PCET are very diverse and therefore using a wide range of resources will engage and motivate them and meet the range of their needs. There are many differences between students that affect their learning. Differentiation is about coping with these differences and using them to promote learning. Differentiated learning takes into account that your students may differ in terms of their motivation, prior experience and knowledge, learning support needs, cultural expectations, literacy, language, numeracy and ICT levels and their learning preferences. It is important to develop resources that cover more than one level of difficulty, use different media or give your students choices of how to complete tasks and provide learning support where necessary.

Differentiation enables all students to participate in learning and reduces the chance of challenging behaviour occurring. This personalisation of learning is very important and ensures that students feel valued and supported. Working in the PCET sector requires a commitment from lecturers to adopt an ethos where every student matters and every student's learning needs are accommodated as far as is practical and possible.

Bees by nature work hard and want to produce the honey; all the bee-keeper needs to do is provide the right environment and the incentive to work hard and the bees will do the rest.

Rewarding success

One of the most useful ways of encouraging good behaviour is to reward good behaviour and encourage and reward achievement.

Each student must be respected and valued for who and what she/he is and a relationship of trust must be built between you and the student. This is expressed by Rogers (1983) as 'unconditional positive regard'. The lecturer must demonstrate unconditional positive regard for each student and this will dispose the student to feel safe and valued, and will improve behaviour. If you are rewarding the student with trust and respect by using praise to reinforce good behaviour then the student is unlikely to want to break that trust by behaving badly.

A number of students in FET have very low self-esteem, so by giving out nuggets of praise when it is warranted we can enhance their feelings of self-worth and competence by acknowledging their good qualities and strengths. Bees will be more productive if they feel secure and safe in the hive. This is down to the relationship with the bee-keeper and the other bees and can be encouraged by patience and care on the part of the bee-keeper.

Relating this analogy specifically to the transitional phases in new educational settings is really important. Making sure that students settle quickly and easily into a new setting is the most important role of the teacher as once they feel safe, valued and happy in the setting they rarely want to leave and are much less likely to want to upset the dynamic by behaving badly and disrupting the rhythm of the class. Bees rarely leave the beehive and work harmoniously with all of the other bees unless badly provoked.

Observation of behaviour for learning in practice

Ofsted's annual reports have highlighted the fact that the behaviour of some students, usually boys (see section below), remains a serious concern for many schools and other settings. Their behaviour troubles others, affects the climate of the learning community and disrupts their own and others' progress.

Throughout your teaching career you will often be observed teaching and one of the key aspects of practice that will strongly influence your grade/outcome will be your approach to managing behaviour and how you deal with any aspects of challenging or disruptive behaviour.

Table 4.1 shows how a judgement might be made and what aspects of behaviour are being scrutinised in the current climate.

Table 4.1 How to manage behaviour effectively to ensure a good and safe learning environment

Manage behaviour effectively to ensure a good and safe learning environment

How well does the teacher:

- Make use of the relevant setting behaviour policy and employ a range of effective strategies to secure appropriate learning behaviour, self-control and independence so that all students can make progress?
- Ensure that students know the boundaries of acceptable behaviour and understand the consequences of their actions?
- Minimise the impact of negative behaviour of some students on teaching and the learning of others?
- Establish and maintain effective relationships in the classroom between teacher and student, other adult and student and student to student?
- Understand the link between students' behaviour and their involvement and engagement with learning?

Evidence may be demonstrated by:

- Planning documentation
  - Effective behaviour for learning strategies used
  - Seating plans and clear classroom routines identified
  - Planning showing the effective use of additional classroom support
  - Planning showing consideration of clear behaviour management strategies
- Reflective documents
  - Evaluations identify future learning targets
  - Awareness of social and emotional factors and cultural and linguistic factors that influence student performance
  - Awareness of wellbeing and resilience building
- Lesson observation shows
  - High expectations and effective and appropriate behaviour management strategies observed
  - Variety of teaching styles, variation of tone and language appropriate to audience
  - Effective relationships with students being developed
  - Good use of humour, praise and formative and summative feedback
  - Setting policies for behaviour used appropriately
  - Records of sanctions and disruptive students maintained

What you can do . . .

- Set and agree ground rules in the first lesson.
- Revisit these ground rules often.
- Ensure you follow through with the agreed consequences every time.
- Ensure you treat everyone fairly.
- Remember to use praise and reward good behaviour.
- Make good use of humour and be relaxed.

- Plan interesting and engaging lessons.
- Avoid any free time in lessons – plan everything.
- Understand your students and their triggers.
- Develop good strong relationships with everyone in the group.
- Remember to stretch and challenge everyone and be aware of the individual learning needs of all students.

Teaching boys

Ofsted highlighted in their recent annual report that bad behaviour was 'usually boys'; however, one of the areas that really needs exploring is how we teach boys and what our expectations of boys in the classroom are. I like to call this behaviour 'boysterous' behaviour as opposed to bad behaviour as a lot of it is down to the nature of boys and the education system as it exists today as opposed to the boys themselves!

Teaching boys is different from teaching girls – it is not worse or better but it is different. In the age range of 14–19 years boys mature at a different rate from girls and their emotional and social development is slower than that of girls of the same age. Most girls will have gone through puberty and all of the difficult emotional issues during their time at school and will join us in our sector already more or less fully mature and developed into the person they will be for the rest of their lives. Boys are not there yet, they will often go through massive physical changes during their time in PCET, often growing much taller and developing into much more physical and mature men. Their emotional development is also being undertaken during this time and they are often struggling to deal with the massive range of emotions they are feeling; however, unlike girls, they are often trying to hide these emotions and to deal with them on their own. It is not 'cool' to show emotion and so this emotion often bursts out and manifests itself as bad behaviour rather than emotional distress. Our job is to try to see through the bravado and to identify the exact trigger for the bad behaviour rather than reacting to the behaviour itself.

Some interesting facts . . .

- Boys tend to be more represented at the very bottom and the very top of achievement.
- Boys are less inclined than girls to learn from indifferent teaching.
- Many schools now use mainly 'girl friendly' assessments.
- Boys are more likely to be influenced by their male peer group that might devalue school work and so put them at odds with academic achievement.
- Boys will do better in education if they have a male primary school teacher.
- 35 per cent of males said having a male teacher challenged them to work harder.
- Only approx. 24 per cent of teachers are male.

- Only approx. 13 per cent of primary teachers are male.
- For many one-parent families, a teacher may be the child's only male role model.
- Boys like clear, focused activities that have a sensible purpose.
- They often hate, and will not engage in, the 'fluffy stuff'.
- Boys like activity – kinaesthetic.
- Boys like a purpose.
- Boys like competition.
- Boys tend not to ask for help.
- Boys can be poor at expressing emotion.
- Boys are more extreme – they get it right or completely wrong.
- Boys take criticism very personally.
- Boys do not take confrontation well.
- Boys are often less developed at this stage as independent students and suffer more from high teacher turnover.

What you can do . . .

- grab students attention
- know their interests and motivators
- put something on in the classroom that is an attention grabber
- use music
- quizzes/puzzles
- brain gym
- use competitions
- allow larger group work
- allow single-gender group work
- realise that boys are more likely to give you credit for trying!
- have a good knowledge of sport, music and TV, which can get you a long way!
- be a good sport and be able to laugh at yourself. This helps to build that relationship!
- Understand that a good relationship is crucial to teaching boys!

This last point is perhaps the most important as that personal relationship should be the cornerstone of your teaching strategies when working with all younger students, but especially with boys. Developing this relationship quickly during the transition phase is very important. If you can establish this relationship in the first couple of weeks then you will ensure you are able to get the best out of these 'boysterous' students and will enjoy the most rewarding of experiences – that of making a difference and changing the life chances of a new generation of boys.

Bullying

All teachers and all schools/colleges have the duty to prevent and tackle all forms of bullying, including homophobic bullying and they cannot discriminate on grounds of sexual orientation or perceived sexual orientation against a student or teacher.

> Education and Inspections Act 2006 – identify and implement measures to promote good behaviour, respect for others and self-discipline amongst pupils and to prevent all forms of bullying.

> Single Equality Act 2010 and Public Duty – schools and other public bodies have to be more proactive and to go beyond non-discrimination by advancing equality.

Bullying is sadly a major part of today's society and is something that every teacher will come across. We have an absolute duty to ensure ALL our students are safe and secure and enjoying their learning and as such MUST always act in any instances of bullying/inappropriate language or behaviour – we must always have a zero tolerance approach to this and then our students will know that we will consistently and fairly follow up any and all instances of bullying and this will enable them to understand and moderate their behaviour.

One of the most frequent manifestations of this is the use of words such as 'gay' in a derogatory and offensive way. It has become common to use 'gay' as an insult and this must always be challenged. It may not be offensive to you or others in the class, but to those struggling with their sexuality it may discourage them from being able to talk about their feelings and worries.

Over the years I have experienced bullying in many forms, both personally and in my twenty-five years of teaching, and I can safely say that bullying can happen to anyone, from any background and with any physical characteristics. It is not only the weak or those who are from minority groups; it can be anyone for any reason – I was bullied for having big ears! It took me years to realise that having ears that stick out slightly is not a major character flaw but just something unique about me! It sounds silly – it is silly – but to my 14 year old self it was very upsetting and traumatising. I always try and remember that 14 year old me who would have willingly had surgery to pin my ears back when I am dealing with any instances of bullying because I can still remember exactly how she felt!

A brief summary of the many types of bullying is shown in figure 4.1.

Some psychological studies highlight characteristics such as low self-esteem as an issue; others suggest that bullies can also be popular classroom leaders. Some show those who have been bullied are more likely to bully. Behaviour is often triggered when a bully feels stress or anxiety, which suggests that the brain's natural impulse for empathy is disrupted in the brain of a bully.

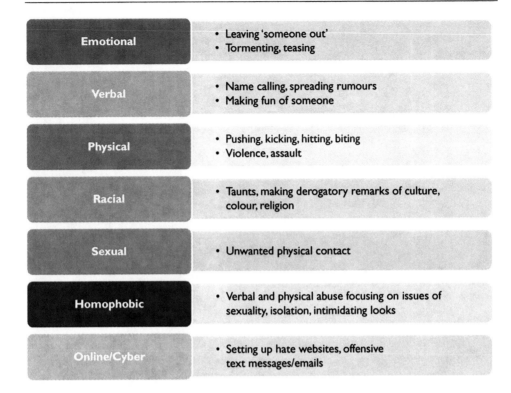

Emotional	• Leaving 'someone out' • Tormenting, teasing
Verbal	• Name calling, spreading rumours • Making fun of someone
Physical	• Pushing, kicking, hitting, biting • Violence, assault
Racial	• Taunts, making derogatory remarks of culture, colour, religion
Sexual	• Unwanted physical contact
Homophobic	• Verbal and physical abuse focusing on issues of sexuality, isolation, intimidating looks
Online/Cyber	• Setting up hate websites, offensive text messages/emails

Figure 4.1 Types of bullying

Not all bullies are the same . . .

- Some bullies simply want power and domination over others.
- Some are seeking to interact with others but lack the skills.
- Some are seeking attention.
- Some are jealous of their victims.
- Many bullies are being bullied themselves.
- Some young people are so worried about being bullied that they become bullies rather than let it happen to them.

Bullying can . . .

- make the lives of victims a misery;
- undermine their confidence and self-esteem;
- destroy their sense of security;

- have a life-long negative impact;
- make it difficult for people to learn;
- have a lasting detrimental effect on their life chances;
- make young people anxious, withdrawn, depressed or aggressive;
- make some turn to substance abuse;
- make some commit suicide.

What you can do . . .

- Create a safe and inclusive environment in which differences and diversity are promoted and celebrated.
- All instances of homophobic/inappropriate language should be challenged and students made to understand why using it is wrong.
- Every incident of bullying should be taken seriously and quickly acted upon.
- Be equipped – access training on how to combat bullying, read the Acceptable Behaviour Policy/Anti-Bullying Policy.
- Encourage role models – demonstrate best practice and use positive role models in your subject area.
- Broaden the curriculum – promote positive images, language e.g. resources.
- Share good practice with colleagues.
- Remember the bigger picture – drive to improve behaviour, boost aspiration, standards and attainment – and of course Ofsted!
- Include a section on bullying in student handbook/induction – signpost Anti-Bullying Policy and procedures.
- Make sure everyone knows what bullying is and what to do if they see it or experience it. A clear consistent response is essential.

The goals of any intervention should always be the same . . .

- to make the victim safe;
- to stop the bullying and change the bully's behaviour;
- to make clear to every student that bullying is unacceptable;
- to learn lessons from the experience that can be applied in future.

If bullying is reported . . .

- The member of staff should immediately investigate.
- Where there is evidence they should contact the anti-bullying lead or Student Services.
- Talk to the student who has been bullied, establish what has happened, and agree a way forward.
- Take bullying seriously and avoid telling students to 'just ignore it'.
- Agree an action plan with his/her consent.

Remember it is always your responsibility to take action and to try to make life easier for the bullied person and to try to change the behaviour of the bully. Bullying may be more common during transitions phases as young people fight for position in the new learning environment and re-invent themselves in this new and changing context.

CASE STUDY 4.1: LEICESTER COLLEGE

The Year 11 Summer Transition Programme was a unique programme for young people vulnerable during transition from school to Leicester College in 2012.

Background

Leicester College is one of the largest in the UK with more than 26,900 students studying on a wide range of courses, from many backgrounds and with different ambitions and aspirations.

We offer hundreds of courses from entry to university level and provide training for thousands of local and national companies. The College has three state-of-the-art city centre campuses and runs courses in more than eighty community venues. We have 670 students studying university-level courses and around 2,000 Apprentices and Advanced Apprentices. 5,900 students study Skills for Life courses with over 800 students going on to Higher Education after studying at Leicester College. We have 400 students aged 14–16 years, and 5,200 students aged 16–18 years.

The College has an annual budget of £54 million. We are members of five National Skills Academy networks in the areas of Food and Drink, Environmental Technologies, Retail, Creative and Cultural and Materials Production and Supply. We have also recently been appointed the East Midlands Hub for The Peter Jones Enterprise Academy.

The College is committed to enriching the lives of all members of the community and to creating new opportunities for them. This is reflected in our mission statement: 'To deliver a wide range of high quality learning experiences to support the diverse communities we serve and the personal, social and economic development of individuals and enterprises'. This driver was the vehicle for us to engage in work to support transition for vulnerable young people from schools to the College.

In the summer of 2012 we carried out work to support students progressing from year 11 from the many feeder schools that span Leicester and Leicestershire, to the College. The European Social Fund (ESF) set up to improve employment opportunities in the European Union and to help raise standards of living was used to fund the programme. ESF aims to help people fulfil their potential by giving them better skills and better job prospects, with a particular focus on the most disadvantaged in the labour market.

We developed a four day programme of activity to serve as early intervention of transition, recognising that for some young people it is the transition process that may form part of the barrier to studying post-16 and that it is the vulnerable students that are at risk of becoming NEET, 'Not in Education, Employment or Training'. With the number of NEETs in the city of Leicester being at an all-time high and growing, this is an area of significant interest.

Progression data tell us that Foundation Level students are less likely to progress to the next level, for example from Level 1 to Level 2. This may suggest that a Foundation Level student is less likely to be sure about their career aims or that they are more likely to change their minds. As Career Learning Information Advice and Guidance continues to be a challenge for us, all new ways of engaging with young people to examine career choices rises on the 14–16 agenda.

Programme

A programme was developed with the aim of meeting the diverse transition needs of vulnerable students. The programme took place on Friday 7th, 14th, 21st and 28th June 2012 from 9 AM until 3 PM. Day one was an introduction to the curriculum area in which the young person had been offered a place for a course starting the following September. Days two to four explored a variety of topics across the different curriculum areas according to the resource available and needs of those attending the programme. These included wide ranging activities such as navigation from one site to another, an introduction to the learning mentors, visits to local employers, assessment of functional skills, assessment of dyslexia, challenging barriers to learning through psychologically based exercises, team building exercises, tasks to challenge perceptions, stretching comfort zones and helping young people to examine the suitability of their choices for post-16 study.

Pilot

106 students were identified during their study in year 11 by the feeder schools in the city and county of Leicestershire and by Connexions Personal Advisors as potentially requiring additional support to sustain a successful transition to the College post-16. All had applied for a course at the College and had been offered a place and thirty-five had studied at the College part time on one of our 14–16 school link programmes. Some of the young people had only visited the College for their interview and had not attended any College open days or engagement activities during years 9, 10 or 11 whilst they were at school.

The vulnerabilities of the young people varied and ranged from confidence issues to disabilities. Detailed information was collected from the schools about the young people so that appropriate support could be arranged.

Results and evaluation

Of the 106 students identified, 68 attended the four day programme. A number of factors contributed to this. In general young people who had been attending the College during the academic year 2011–12 on 14–16 part time programmes chose not to attend. We are able to ascertain this as these young people made a positive transition to the college in September 2012 despite not having attended the transition programme, demonstrating they were able to assess their own need and suitability for such a course. In addition, attendance was affected by Awarding Organisations externally set examinations, some of which fell on the dates of the transition programme. Young people at entry and Level 1 that had limited experience of the College and had no examinations on the programme dates demonstrated the best attendance on the programme.

Feedback on the value of the programme was gained from Leicester College staff, Connexions Personal Advisors, students and their parents. In particular the comments from young people were very positive: 'I felt really happy for the whole summer knowing what I was coming to in September' and 'I was scared before I came to the College, the course helped me settle in' were comments from two young people. Evaluations also helped to explain in further detail the aspects of the programme that were most beneficial. Becoming familiar with the College and the staff, the pastoral elements and the navigation that impacted transition took precedence rather than the curriculum ingredient. The feedback has now been cross-referenced to the destinations data of the selected cohort. This demonstrates that the insecurities and vulnerabilities of the young people were varied, that they perceived the programme as beneficial and that it helped them to progress and to succeed in the very important transition from key stage 4.

Some young people used this experience and process as a vehicle to change their post 16 choice of study. Some realigned their interest to another strand of the same vocation, from painting and decorating to plumbing for example, and some to a completely different vocational area. Others used it to reaffirm their choices.

Of the sixty-eight students who attended the programme 75 per cent enrolled at the College and the remaining 25 per cent of young people progressed either to another post-16 provider or into work. This showed that 100 per cent of students that attended the transition programme made a positive progression in September 2012.

Young people that attended one, two or three days of the transition programme also made a successful transition to the College and their attendance duration appears not to have impacted on their final progression. This demonstrates that a shorter programme may also be successful.

This pilot sought to improve transition and progression for young people vulnerable during transition from leaving school to starting at the College, and was successful. The College views this as the start of very necessary engagement and will use the lessons learned from this as a foundation to build future transition programmes upon.

Chapter 5

Developing independence and motivating learning using a coaching and mentoring approach

Identify nature of coaching and mentoring and link to key aspects of independence and motivation

The aim of this chapter is to consider the essence of coaching and mentoring and explore ways that it can be used to establish and promote independence and motivation amongst our learners.

The historical perspective of mentoring is well documented with its roots in Homer's epic poem, the *Odyssey*. Whilst there is debate about the nature of mentoring portrayed in the *Odyssey*, the interpretation offered by Garvey *et al.* (2009: 12) is one 'based on experiential learning with support and challenge', a view supported by Megginson and Clutterbuck (2005) and Connor and Pokora (2012). Indeed, it could be argued that there is an emerging focus on the common ground between coaching and mentoring, rather than deliberation over the differences. This is a constructive approach for our purposes. The use of coaching and mentoring to establish a learning relationship (Connor and Pokora 2012) that fosters independence, realisation of potential and a clearer sense of direction is one that resonates with the learner-centred approach that characterises much outstanding practice in the post-compulsory sector. The concept of a developmental relationship (Megginson and Clutterbuck 2005: 4) in which performance improvement (coaching) is linked effectively with 'the identification and nurturing of potential for the whole person' (mentoring) offers a symbiotic relationship that may be used for the continuing benefit of each learner.

Brockbank and McGill (2012) acknowledge the confusion that remains around the interchangeable terminology of coaching and mentoring but offer a route to clarification by relating practice to three key questions: Whose purpose? What process? Which learning outcome? This is a particularly useful approach if we are seeking to foster in our learners skills that will build resilience, impetus and momentum, factors vital in facilitating effective transition between education phases and enhanced employability. The goal of developmental interaction is for the learner to take responsibility for their own learning and development, but it offers the potential for longer-term benefits. Transformation of familiar thought processes through reflective dialogue encourages new perspectives. However, whilst intrapersonal reflection is an integral part of personal and professional development, it requires effective use of a range of higher order thinking skills. Brockbank and McGill (2012: 46, original emphasis) argue that this approach is *'ultimately not enough to promote transformational learning*'. Instead, they propose that interpersonal reflection within a coaching or mentoring relationship 'guarantees that learners are challenged, that double loop learning is an option and that the transformational learning which results from dialogue is a real potential outcome'. Engagement, inclusion, purpose and support are characteristics of reflective dialogue and essential if transformation is to be achieved.

The concept of permanent change through a coaching relationship is a common thread that runs through much of the associated literature. A vital part of our role as practitioners is to widen our understanding and responsibility towards learners in enabling and equipping them to learn. Whitmore (2009: 10) encapsulates this view in his definition: 'Coaching is unlocking people's potential to maximise their own performance. It is helping them to learn rather than teaching them.' This interpretation resonates with Rosinski's view (cited by Passmore 2010: 10) that defines coaching as 'the art of facilitating the unleashing of people's potential to reach meaningful, important objectives'. Underpinning this is an inherent belief in the potential of others and a commitment to the process of discovery. Lack of self-belief, fear of failure and lack of confidence are common barriers to realisation of potential. However, a growth mindset will sustain an optimistic approach and uses opportunities for learners to make decisions, take responsibility, explore options and take action. It is Whitmore's assertion that constructing the self-belief of others, heedless of circumstances, is fundamental to coaching. He advocates the assimilation of this philosophy to our way of thinking and being and relating to one another.

If such approaches are to be used effectively as agents of change with our learners, then it is of vital importance that the professional development of teachers as outstanding practitioners is supported by an organisational culture permeated by the principles of coaching and mentoring. In their extensive and influential work on the links between staff development and student learning, Joyce and Showers (2002) analyse case studies where professional communities have had a significant impact on students' learning. They suggest that there are four key components to staff training: developing knowledge of new skills and strategies through exploration of underpinning principles, concept and theory; the demonstration or modelling of new skills; practice of the skill; and peer coaching. Furthermore, they emphasise the fact that training programmes that included all four aspects were notably more effective than those that included single factors or, indeed, the first three but not peer coaching.

Joyce and Showers identified five ways in which coaching influenced the transfer of learning. It appears that practitioners for whom coaching had been an integral part of the learning/developmental process felt able to practise strategies more often and more skilfully than colleagues who had not had the benefit of coaching. They were also able to adapt the strategies more easily to respond to the needs of their own context and sustained the new skills over a longer period of time. Interestingly, coached practitioners were also more likely to articulate the rationale underpinning the new strategies and, finally, they exhibited a depth and clarity of understanding of the intended outcome of the new strategies. The researchers concluded that this was the result of frequent opportunities for peer discussion that encouraged and facilitated critical thinking around new strategies. Cox (2013: 139) explores the concept of coaching transfer, citing perspectives offered by Stewart *et al.*, who refer to it as 'the sustained application of the knowledge, skills, attitudes and other qualities gained during coaching, into the workplace', and Súilleabháin and Sime, who argue that it is 'the influence of prior learning on new contexts of learning or performance'. The ability to transfer learning between contexts, identified as 'far transfer' (Perkins and Saloman; cited by Cox 2013) in contrast to 'near transfer', prompts consideration of the need to ensure that approaches to coaching provide learners with the ability and confidence to apply new skills in a range of different situations. The key factor is the ability of the practitioner to act independently and, it could be argued, realise the motivation to do so. Cox develops this argument, using Lobato's 'actor-oriented approach' that involves analysis of the learner's knowledge and performance and determination of the extent to which they are able transfer these to effective participation in activity in a different situation. This has significant implications both for development of professional practice amongst practitioners and for the strengthening of transferable skills that facilitate transition between phases for students. However, it should be acknowledged that learners may experience feelings of uncertainty, 'disorienting dilemma', and questioning of beliefs and assumptions in the initial phases of transformation (Mezirow; cited by Cox 2013). It appears that the integration of coaching into the equation has the potential not simply to reproduce knowledge and skills but to transform participation in multiple situations. This is fundamental to fostering confident, independent and self-reliant learners who are able to apply their knowledge, skills and identity (Cox 2013) in different contexts, thus enhancing opportunities for progression and employability.

This reinforces the importance of creating a coaching culture within the organisation. According to a survey of organisations in the Education and Skills sector by the Learning and Skills Improvement Service (LSIS) (Turner 2012), 66 per cent of respondents provide internal coaching and 57 per cent advocate higher levels of coaching qualifications. In an article examining the response to major change in the sector, Turner (2012: 12) identifies the positive impact that coaching has had both on a one-to-one basis and as a leadership style: 'It provides the support and clarity of thinking needed to help learning providers thrive, making a difference to leadership, organisations and the classroom'; she cites improved observation grades, improved targets setting by students, improved morale and changing culture as manifestations of this impact. Furthermore, 100 per cent of respondents felt that coaching was at least as effective as other change interventions and it was 'also seen to have a direct, very positive impact on teaching and learning as well as on leadership and management'. The development of coaching at Shrewsbury College was the focus of a case study that formed part of the research carried out by LSIS. Turner uses the findings of the case study to illustrate the impact of coaching on key indicators within the College. A coaching approach was embedded into the organisation's strategic plan and supported by a commitment by the Senior Management Team to fund the initiative. The impact was transformational, facilitating fundamental change at different levels throughout the College. In terms of performance, 80 per cent of staff who received coaching, individually or in groups, improved their observation grades; improvement for those who had not received coaching was just under 7 per cent.

It is apparent that there are close links between a strong coaching culture within an organisation and the positive and potentially far-reaching effects that this can have on both staff and students, particularly through periods of significant change. However, it is important to consider the business case for coaching and to acknowledge the cost of commitment to such an initiative. Clarity of vision and strategy, supported by rigorous and responsive monitoring of impact, is essential.

Characteristics of coaching and mentoring

The principles of growth, development and release of potential form the framework of several models of coaching; Connor and Pokora (2012) relate them to the learning relationship as the core element of effective practice. Indeed, Cox (2013: 159) emphasises the importance of coaches as learning specialists who are able to foster self-direction and criticality. Coaching as a form of learning (Starr 2011) reflects the co-created impetus required to catalyse learning and self-development; movement is an inherent characteristic. Downey (2003) illustrates how crucial a belief in learning is to the facilitation of potential. He describes a coaching skills workshop in which the participants were improving their ball-catching skills. The volunteer, Peter, described in this episode demonstrated lack of confidence and self-belief, confessing that he had never been able to catch a ball. The coach continued to throw a ball to Peter, each time asking a question that encouraged him to focus on the ball as it approached; he caught five of the eight balls thrown to him after initially failing to catch any. As Peter overcame his fear of failure and self-doubt, he was able to access his natural ability and learn quickly. The coach seemingly did very little but the episode serves to demonstrate clearly the link between coaching and effective teaching and learning through facilitation. Downey (2003) argues that effective coaching can bring about fulfilment, in which he includes learning and development, and that learners can experience work in a meaningful sense through enhancement of intrinsic motivation. This approach has the potential to inspire learners who, strengthened by experience and success, are better equipped to welcome responsibility and demonstrate independence.

Effective coaching is based on key principles; Starr (2011) asserts that these include commitment to support of the individual, shared honesty and trust, a belief in potential for achievement beyond that which is currently apparent, and the responsibility of the coachee for the outcome of the coaching process. These are congruent with the characteristics of outstanding teaching and learning; as practitioners we seek to create learning experiences for our students that are based on a growth mindset, confident that each individual student has the capacity to advance beyond prevailing horizons. Essential to this is a non-judgemental attitude; objectivity reflected in a neutral and open approach can encourage sharing of relevant thoughts and feelings. This is an important factor in the coaching relationship and a milestone towards creating a sense of responsibility in our students.

> In coaching, this sense of an individual's personal responsibility is key if we are to empower them to act powerfully and positively in their situation. It is useful to break the word responsibility into two halves, as it literally becomes 'response' and 'ability' – in other words, the ability to respond.
>
> (Starr 2011: 37)

This further strengthens the case for coaching as a significant intervention in developing independent and self-reliant learners who are better prepared to meet the challenges inherent in change and transition.

As the relationship that teachers have with their learners is fundamental to the success of the learning process, so is the coaching relationship with learners. Power rests neither with coach nor learner but in the relationship created between the two (Claridge and Lewis 2005). The impact of effective questioning is not easily overestimated; curiosity questioning in which the coach suspends judgement invites the learner to embark upon a journey and provides 'leverage for change' (Claridge and Lewis 2005: 6). Whitmore (2009) believes that the effect coaches strive to create is one of awareness and responsibility and that this is achieved through asking effective questions. The intention of this approach is not for the coach to glean information, but rather to ascertain that the coachee recognises that they have the information and to provide a springboard for subsequent questions in pursuit of a constructive outcome. Open questions using words like what, when, who and how much cultivate awareness but Whitmore (2009: 47) cautions against using why as it may imply criticism and can provoke defensiveness. Interestingly, he links why and how, suggesting that, if unqualified, they can cause analytical thinking that may be detrimental: 'Analysis (thinking) and awareness (observation) are dissimilar mental modes that are virtually impossible to employ simultaneously to full effect'. Instead, he proposes that why questions are rephrased in terms such as 'What were the reasons . . .?' and *how* questions as 'What are the steps . . .?' An increasing focus on detail will encourage the learner to draw into focus factors hitherto concealed in the subconscious. An effective coach will use any uncertainty and confusion to advantage, encourage the learner to consider options, assess outcomes and prioritise actions; in essence, create a learning opportunity. Whitmore (2009: 41) distils these functions, suggesting that the coach plays several roles: 'a sounding board, a facilitator, a counsellor, an awareness raiser'.

Explore different models of coaching through transition

Transition is the process or a period of changing from one state or condition to another. Bridges (2009) distinguishes between change and transition, asserting that transition is more complex as it implies new ways of thinking and behaving and is generally more protracted. Transition involves three phases: endings (letting go), neutral zone (finding meaning) and beginnings (moving on). Paradoxically, the model starts with an ending and ends with a beginning. Understanding the complexity of this process and supporting the emotions associated with disorientation, low motivation and high anxiety that may be involved in transition are fundamental to supporting learners through periods of change. The psychological process of adaptation to change is also reflected in Scott and Jaffe's Change Model (1995). This too acknowledges and assimilates the impact of change on thoughts and emotions and considers causal links with the disempowerment and re-empowerment aspects of the change process. There are several models and conceptual frameworks used in a coaching relationship to facilitate and accomplish change. Used appropriately and sensitively, they can lend structure to learning conversations but should not be superimposed on the process to the detriment of the learner's needs.

The importance of awareness and responsibility raised by Whitmore (2009) is reflected in the nature of the benefits that ensue from these concepts. As we strive to establish and nurture independence and motivation in our learners there is exciting potential in the concept of responsibility that can inspire uniqueness, self-esteem and ownership that, in turn, engender potential, confidence and self-motivation. The GROW model proposed by Whitmore (2009: 55) provides a structure and sequence of questions under four headings:

- **Goal** setting for the session as well as short and long term.
- **Reality** checking to explore the current situation.
- **Options** and alternative strategies or courses of action.
- **What** is to be done, **When**, by **Whom**, and the **Will** to do it.

The model can be used flexibly, particularly over a course of coaching sessions, either on a one-to-one basis or as a strategy used by a practitioner with a group of staff or students. One of the advantages of aspiring to long term goal setting is that it can be used to inspire learners to consider ideal scenarios that are not diluted by established patterns of behaviour or thought. Learners can be encouraged to visualise long term goals in terms of career prospects that may involve transition from one study phase, organisational setting or peer group to another. Coaching has the capacity to transform negative emotions and perspectives associated with past experience and performance (fixed mindset) to a strengthened belief in personal potential, curiosity and excitement about opportunities and commitment to courses of action (growth mindset). The GROW model offers a framework in which to explore options and the freedom to move forward; in the process the learner has started to develop the thinking skills required to be an independent learner, increasingly aware of and able to use the metacognitive skills which are fundamental to sustained growth.

Through the Solutions Focus, Jackson and McKergow (2007: xv) propound 'a powerful, practical and proven approach to positive change with people, teams and organizations'. This radically simple approach enables learners to

> sidestep the often fruitless search for the causes of problems, take the direct route forwards and simply head straight for the solution. The focus on solutions (not problems), strengths (not weaknesses), and on what's going well (rather than what's gone wrong) leads to a positive and pragmatic way of making progress.

This is an attractive perspective; it acknowledges the perpetual nature of change, embraces different views and places positive thinking at the heart of the process. The roots of Solutions Focus emanate from psychotherapy and, in common with coaching, use purposeful conversations as the foundation for growth and change.

Solutions-focused coaching uses OSKAR as a framework; the acronym representing five phases: Outcome, Scaling, Know-how, Affirm and action, Review. The initial outcome phase is used to determine the needs of the learner and uses questions such as 'What do you want to achieve today?', 'What do you want to achieve in the long term?' and the future perfect to encourage the learner to visualise the scenario and be motivated by their capacity to achieve all or part of it. The scaling tool that follows this stage is a powerful agent for change. It stimulates consideration of where the learner is at present in terms of knowledge or levels of confidence or commitment or it may reflect alternative perspectives. It is important for the learner to discover the know-how for themselves and encourages them to explore similar experiences or achievements and the resources required to succeed. During the affirmation stage, it is important for the coach to recognise positive steps forward and qualities in the learner that could accelerate progress. The process of reflecting this back to the learner immediately precedes identification of further action. It can be useful to refer to the scaling activity and, crucially, ask the learner what action they could take that would move them one step on the scale. Small steps are essential and more effective if the learner is able to describe how they would know they had successfully taken the next step. Review may reflect on progress to date but may also project forward to the subsequent session, using a cyclical process to reinforce the impact of actions taken by the learner.

The Leicester College case study was based on a Summer Transition Programme aimed at young people vulnerable during transition from school to Leicester College in 2012. Prompted by concern about an increasing number of young people in the NEET category, the College developed a four day programme of activity to serve as early intervention of transition, recognising that for some young people it is the transition process that may form part of the barrier to studying post-16. Participants were invited to attend on four Fridays in June 2012; the first day was an introduction to the curriculum area in which the learner had chosen to study and the three subsequent days provided opportunities to explore a variety of topics within the curriculum area. The second phase included environmental orientation, introduction to learning mentors, visits to employers, assessment of Functional Skills and team building exercises.

Of the 106 learners identified, 68 attended the four day programme. Attendance was affected by the decision taken by learners already studying at the College not to attend the programme and the impact of externally set exams, some of which coincided with the transition days. Subsequent evaluation of the programme demonstrated that 'insecurities and vulnerabilities of the young people were varied, that they perceived the programme as beneficial and that it helped them to progress and to succeed in the very important transition from key stage 4'. Crucially, however, 'of the 68 learners who attended the programme, 75 per cent enrolled at the College and the remaining 25 per cent of young people progressed either to another post-16 provider or in to work. This showed that 100 per cent of learners that attended the transition programme made a positive progression in September 2012.' The College concluded that the pilot study that had been designed to improve transition and progression for vulnerable young people had been successful and plans to develop this initiative further.

This chapter has explored the nature of coaching and mentoring and the impact that implementation of effective practice may have on the development of independence and motivation of learners. It has considered the opportunities created by an organisational culture that embraces coaching and mentoring as key to the professional development of practitioners as only then are they able to appreciate the benefits of incorporating this philosophy as an integral part of their engagement with learners. Further investigation into the nature of change and transition has revealed the complex interaction of thought, emotion and perception that takes place as we move from one phase to another. Closer analysis of models of coaching has provided insight into possible frameworks that could be used to facilitate transition. However, they provide opportunities to achieve more than this. Thoughtful, committed, intuitive and focused use of coaching techniques has the capacity to build independence in our learners, to provide them with skills associated with effective progression and ongoing recognition and achievement of potential.

Part 2

Teaching, learning and assessment

Chapter 6

The planning cycle

This chapter looks critically at planning to inclusively meet the needs of students in transition and to allow them to develop the skills of purposeful enquiry and self-directed learning. Teachers and lecturers are therefore encouraged to reflect on their existing practice and to become educational practitioners who are fully aware of their students and their needs particularly during transitions. A fundamental yet essential consideration of inclusivity during transition is that all students are entitled to learn in environments that take into account *how* they learn and *how* they are taught. It is extremely problematic if an attempt is made to be prescriptive about the ways in which any institution or setting supports individual students. It is clear from our experiences, observations and research however (Bostock and Wood 2011, 2012), that there are generalisable elements of best practice that can promote their wellbeing, increase the likelihood of success and achievement, and maximise personal, academic or vocational development. Education, at all levels in the UK, has undergone immense transformation since the Further and Higher Education Acts of 1992. While many gains have been made, it is generally recognised that the country's challenge of under-preparation for transition to university for instance is not a new phenomenon. However, given the enormous educational transformations that have taken place, this issue has become more salient over the past ten years and a range of interventions have been put in place by universities to attempt to support new students. These interventions include bridging and foundation programmes, university entrance tests, and academic support integrated within degree programmes. These measures are of course only accessible once students are officially part of the university. We need to consider support which transcends the perceived divides between secondary, tertiary and higher education.

Fortunately, transition in education at any level benefits from an established and wide ranging literature that includes transition for young people into education and transition between educational institutions. We outlined our theoretical standpoints in chapter 1, but further focus on the concept of CoP will enable a deeper appreciation of the super complexity of transition. Predictably, starting at a new educational institution will involve multiple changes: physical location, peer relationships, social and academic expectations and levels of control. So we provide three examples that could typify transitional key points in the students' journeys. In this and subsequent chapters we will first explore and review three overarching transition stages, namely: moving from a school to a college, moving through college and starting university. We then propose numerous and diverse strategies, tasks and activities to support students that we feel can be applied to any of the stages. Whilst we acknowledge just three stages that individuals in transition must manage, we do, however, endeavour to understand both practically and theoretically the multiple transition trajectories by emphasising the shifts in identity through each transition to plan for smoother and more supportive trajectories. The needs and interests of students must be considered and used by the teacher or lecturer to inform planning. As Postance notes: 'Systematic planning is crucial if the delivered curriculum is to meet the needs of all learners' (in Fawbert 2008: 67). Both the teacher and the student have specific but varied and connected roles that converge in the learning environment or space.

Trajectories into new Communities of Practice (CoPs)

A key factor in understanding transition was outlined in chapter 1 that we maintained is a 'trajectory' into the new CoP. Wenger (1998) identifies different forms of trajectory, which provide interesting characterisations of students in transition:

- Peripheral trajectories – trajectories that do not lead to full participation but do involve identity shifts.
- Inbound trajectories – trajectories that suggest the goal of full participation, even when the participant is peripheral in the beginning.
- Insider trajectories – even when a full participant, practice and meaning and therefore identity can shift.
- Boundary trajectories – those that span a number of CoPs, linking them and brokering practices with them.
- Outbound trajectories – trajectories that clearly enable participation in a future community of practice.

Identity is not, in this theoretical perspective, a stable or static notion. Instead Wenger (1998) proposed that:

- Identity is fundamentally temporal.
- The work of identity is ongoing.
- Because it is constructed in social contexts, the temporality of identity is more complex than a linear notion of time.
- Identities are defined with respect to the interaction of multiple convergent and divergent trajectories.

To further understand the transition of students it is possible to relate the experiences and trajectories to CoPs. CoPs as a theoretical concept is a challenge to traditional transmission models of learning and it is in understanding its notions of practice and participation that the tasks of transition can be more clearly elucidated. In theoretical terms, practices that serve to define a community are constituted by and constitute the participants. The community is dynamic and the members are developing continually as practices evolve. CoPs do not have practices that are rigidly set in stone, which new members acquire and perform. Rather, in performance the practices are reconstituted and in new membership the practices are developed. To that extent students belong to multiple CoPs and all have a range of different practices that they bring to any situation and these practices are negotiated. In such negotiations participation is a wholly social endeavour; in essence it is an exchange. In transition, students are joining new communities and theoretically, by using Wenger's identifications of identity as a referent, they are legitimate peripheral participants in those new communities. In other words, as indicated earlier, their identity is shifting. What does this shifting mean in terms of planning? Before looking at this more closely it will be prudent to briefly review and explain our previous ideas around formulating objectives and in particular how each can be applied to a different theoretical learning domain but with subtle yet very specific differences (see table 6.1). Effective planning for learning involves formulating learning objectives that provide activities to help students meet these objectives to achieve their fullest potential. There are numerous literary references to these formulations (Bostock and Wood 2012; Postance 2008; Armitage *et al.* 2007; Stapleton 2001) and an emphasis on the process of learner interaction and involvement that awards creativity and self-reliance as well as an emphasis on the product of education; that is, academic achievements. In other words opportunities are created for students to be involved in the decisions about what is to be learned and how this is addressed.

In other words we should ask 'Who are the students?' Postance (2008) provides an excellent premise on which to build an understanding of the purpose of planning:

> The key to the whole process is *resonance* rather than prescription. We need to spend time getting to know the learners well and attuning ourselves to their wavelength so that we are able to understand most of the subtle signals that are transmitted between the students and the teacher. Once we have the ability and the motivation to accurately read how the majority of our learners are receiving both the taught material *and the manner in which it is being presented*, our planning and preparation will inevitably begin to have much greater accuracy and meaning.
>
> (in Fawbert 2008: 93, original emphasis)

Table 6.1 Examples of verbs using Bloom's taxonomy

Verb	Cognitive	Affective	Psychomotor
State	Remembering that which has been learned	Ability to participate and react	Ability to know the simple, related steps of a skill
Write	Remembering that which has been learned	Ability to participate and react	Ability to perform literacy based tasks
Find	Remembering that which has been learned	Ability to develop a consistent system of values	Ability to know the simple, related steps of a skill

Source: Bloom (1964).

The metaphor of scaffolding and implications in planning for student transitions

There is much use (and misuse) of the term and metaphor of scaffolding. However, we appreciate its major significance in effective transition. Wood *et al.* (1976), for example, introduced the term in the context of the analysis of adult–child interaction. Stapleton (2001) identified scaffolding as a process in which, via language, a more able or competent person may impart knowledge and understanding to a less able person but in so doing provides a framework within which learners can learn effectively for themselves. This bore clear parallels to Vygotsky's Zone of Proximal Development (ZPD) and has since become synonymous with the process of adult–child interaction within ZPD (Forman *et al.* 1993). In essence Berk and Winsler (1995) also concede that the metaphor of scaffolding requires that the teacher provides relevant and meaningful tasks to assist or facilitate in the extending or stretching of the learners' abilities with a view to encouraging and promoting autonomy. But the emphasis must be on interpersonal activity concentrating on what the learner can do through assistance rather than alone, in other words allowing learners to accomplish tasks not otherwise possible without this intervention. This reciprocal instruction engages students in processes where the teacher can identify discrepancies within the initial stages of learning and thus in the outcomes thereof. Scaffolding has implications for student transitions and the modification needed to maintain optimal levels of challenge (and motivation). This strategy requires the encouraging of active peer collaboration giving rise to the notions of dialogue and its importance in cognitive development. So within this reciprocal instruction, scaffolding requires the instructor to constantly appraise the learners' level of ability. Specifically, successful scaffolding would require a number of functions, amongst which are the selection, organisation and presentation of suitable tasks. These tasks should allow for the teaching of emerging skills, ongoing evaluation of the tasks suitable to their purpose, the generation and maintenance of the learners' interest in the tasks and the clarification of goals. Earlier the interpersonal and dialogic implications of scaffolding were mentioned because above all Vygotsky stresses the centrality of 'language' to cognitive development. Language arises initially as a means of communication between the child and the people in its environment. Only subsequently, upon conversion to internal speech, does it come to organise the child's thought, that is to say, become an internal mental function (Vygotsky 1978). Therefore thinking arises through the internalisation of social activities and events which in stages form part of the individual's mental structures. This can be mediated by:

1   assistance provided by more capable others e.g. teachers, peers;
2   assistance provided by the individual talking aloud (i.e. intrapersonal dialogue);

and

3   internalisation of the concept.

To sum up, language plays a vital role in the evolution of concepts and the nature of scaffolding is the promotion of collaborative problem solving and self-regulation with constant awareness of the learning environment and the need to adjust, intervene and evaluate that provision in order to promote positive and meaningful outcomes. When planning for learning, a variety of factors that can have either a positive or negative impact must be considered e.g. prior experiences, resources, ethnicity, gender, special educational needs. At first this can be very daunting for even the most experienced teacher or lecturer but this can be alleviated when teaching strategies are considered that are flexible, adaptive or differentiated. Stradling and Saunders have previously suggested five types of differentiation that are a useful referent in planning principally associated with either task, outcome, activity, pace and dialogue (1993: 129). This, they argue, can only be successfully implemented if the teacher has a thorough knowledge of the cohorts' needs and learning preferences. Consequently this also involves intricate knowledge on the part of the teacher or lecturer gleaned through an artefact such as a detailed cohort analysis, for example, coupled with a clear overview of what they expect of the students. In addition to these data, for us a rather formulaic but useful axiom around session plan design for learning is:

- Aims and Objectives PLUS Teacher and Student Activity PLUS Assessment = Learning.

Another rather formulaic but useful axiom around preparing and planning for teaching is:

- Scheme of Work PLUS Cohort Analysis PLUS Session Plan = Teaching.

Some of the sorts of activities within subject or programme areas at all levels that might be used to facilitate effective transitions are listed below:

- 'getting to know each other' icebreakers
- addressing anxieties
- group exercises
- social events
- outings – possibly arranged by the students
- a subject area society.

The involvement of current students acting as academic mentors works best around an activity that is thematically linked to typical transition points and experiences; for example, current students introducing a section about things they found helpful in their first week/first term or semester, sharing computing knowledge and introducing the VLE (virtual learning environment) as a repository and more importantly an interactive learning and teaching platform. Subject relevant student clubs, email discussion groups, discussion boards, launching an introductory blog on the VLE, sporting and other activities within the Students' Union can build stronger relationships and encourage effective transition. We shall look more closely at these and other activities on pages 77–87.

Language and context

Further scrutiny of the diversity of students, their contexts and conditions would now be beneficial to further enhance the capacity to plan effectively for learning and teaching. Admittedly first impressions are crucial during any period of transition, so ensuring that all material is accurate, inclusive and up to date, highlighting recent changes so students are aware their programmes are organic and developing rather than static is extremely helpful. Yet this can be problematic and not straightforward. Sometimes our language is so much part of our everyday discourse, we forget that for new students (and sometimes current ones) we need to explain the often-confusing language and terminology associated within subject and professional disciplines. This is viewed by us as an essential part of the induction into any community of practice. Adopting a particular theoretical stance around discourse we consider and agree with discursive analyst and proponent of theories concerning language and context James Gee (2004, 2005) when he states that words and their meanings are never neutral; instead language is the product of a way of living or way of behaving and performing in the world. Each way of behaving or living produces its own language. It is only within a context that we can understand the meaning of words; but when we look for a word's meaning we do not abstract it from a given context and generalise as if there were some essence to be discovered; instead, we look to the way the community of people use such words. Language can say many things simultaneously and therefore it is when there is mutual understanding between communities and individuals that effective communication takes place. Acronyms and specific language terms can be effectively addressed, introducing students to the terminology section on a subject community site (see 'Helping students find their way around', pp. 82–84). This then provides a 24/7 reference guide for them and can be highlighted at any point throughout a programme or course of study.

Transition from school to college

Transition from one learning environment to another has always been a particularly problematic feature of FET which is an all-encompassing acronym for post-secondary institutions of learning. This section will, therefore, explore how this transition is possibly more acutely felt by the 14–16 year old, particularly, if they are more 'vocationally oriented' or have been 'spoon-fed' at school. In 2009 *The Independent* ran a report that contained remarks from the Higher Education Academy that stated 'Higher Education Authority (HEA) chief executive Tom Boland said there is "alarm" at the extent to which the second-level school system is producing students who "learn to the test". These students are then going on to third level where they are expecting the same spoon feeding' (Walshe 2009, updated 2012).

We accept the contentious nature of both these assertions and terms and we do not wish to suggest an acknowledgement that these are generalisable concepts. We do acknowledge, however, how practitioners who have contributed to our research consistently use these terms to identify certain student types as perceived by them.

So questions to ask ourselves will be: what are the learning and teaching approaches that may help us in our planning for learning? In all we will look at how to plan for an effective and productive learning environment for all students and discuss the role of the teacher or lecturer. In the next sections we review and analyse case studies and document types that will be useful in the organisation of planning for learning for those teachers who are involved in teaching recent school leavers.

Scheme of Work (SoW)

There are many definitions of what constitute a Scheme of Work (SoW) (see Minton 2005: 47–57, Postance 2008: 72–78, Armitage *et al.* 2007: 93 and 220–223).

BOX 6.1 A COURSE DESCRIPTION: EXAMPLE OF A SCHEME OF WORK

This is a communicative Level 3 course in French which forms a link between GCSE and A2 Level.

The 4 language skills of listening, speaking, reading and writing are all practised and regularly assessed throughout the course.

From 2009 onwards, the new exam specification places a far greater emphasis than before on grammatical accuracy. In light of this change, the scheme of work has been re-written to reflect the need for students to be able to handle complex grammar.

In addition, from 2009, there is no longer a requirement for students to recall facts about French/French-speaking countries. They may choose to refer to these countries in their essays and oral exams, but will not be penalised for factual inaccuracies.

The element of listening via individual practice on the language lab has been greatly reduced from 2009, with the skill of listening assessed mainly via the oral exam.

General aims of the course or programme

- To produce confident communicators with a good grasp of oral and written language.
- To provide a sound grammatical basis for further study, at A2 level and beyond.
- To explore themes relevant to their lives via the target language, using examples from French life and culture.

- Content/Learning Outcomes
- Teaching and Learning Strategies
- Resources
- Assessment
- Evaluation

Number of students on census' date

- % Retention Rate
- % Achievement Rate
- % Success Rate
- % Average Attendance

The SoW is a working document and its key elements may be subject to amendments in response to any of the following:

- learners' needs, ability levels and preferred learning styles. Timings and methods may change to facilitate revision, reinforcement and extension;
- college priorities, directives, policy development e.g. changes to exam dates;
- any changes to the students' learning programme.

The above ancillary data help the teacher or lecturer gain a consolidated overview of the aims of the course or programme. This can be supplemented very well with details of each individual student ordinarily identified as a cohort analysis.

Cohort analysis

Cristina, a coordinator of Level 3 language programmes and a teaching and learning coach in the FE sector provides an interesting example of a cohort analysis document.

BOX 6.2   A COHORT ANALYSIS DOCUMENT

Please provide a short pen portrait of each student. Include any additional information you think it would be helpful for the observer/inspector to know. Please relate students to the differentiated learning outcomes.

E.g. progress students are making, preferred ways of learning, receiving additional learning support etc.

This is a very small group with just 3 students on roll. They are part of a bigger group and French is one of their 6 subjects plus 2 others.

Erica

Erica is an extremely able student in all subjects who takes her studies very seriously, despite family issues. She genuinely enjoys the French language and has made very good progress since starting the programme. She has a good grasp of grammar, and is able to manipulate advanced tenses in her written essays and when speaking. Erica is very modest and sometimes appears nervous when speaking, having said this she always contributes well to class discussions with some very valid points. Her focus at the moment is to improve pronunciation on particular sounds and to pay more attention to accuracy in verbs in the past tense. She is predicted a high grade for this subject.

Elisabeth

Elisabeth is a natural linguist who genuinely enjoys learning languages in general. Elisabeth is an international student who has travelled, lived and studied in various countries in Europe. English is her third language.

Elisabeth is performing consistently well. Her knowledge of Spanish and Catalan also helps her to understand a wide range of vocabulary and structures. Elisabeth is always focused and committed to her studies, arriving well prepared and participating well in group and paired activities. Elisabeth has made very good progress and she has now the knowledge and ability to apply complex grammatical structures in her written and oral work. She needs to focus in her oral presentation to make sure that her pronunciation is accurate and that she demonstrates a wide range of vocabulary.

Philomena

Philomena is a pleasant student who is very committed to her studies and clearly enjoys the subject. She is hard working and motivated during class time. However, she has recently had some personal problems that have affected her attendance and her concentration in class. This said she is committed to the subject and her language skills show that she can communicate verbally and in writing with increasing accuracy, using a wide range of vocabulary. She needs now to focus on using a wide range of vocabulary and accuracy in her masculine and feminine words.

Once established within a college programme of academic or vocational study it is prudent to establish how planning for learning is still of paramount importance as students work through their programme. Using Wenger's descriptors, it is useful to view students' identities in this instance as comprising inward and outward trajectories. In other words, a shift to new practices and demands within the college setting and a marked increase in preparation for joining a brand new CoP – i.e. the next year up or university. In the next sections we review and analyse case studies and strategies that are useful in the organisation of planning for learning for those teachers who are involved in teaching college students mid-way through a programme of study. Janet, who is head of inclusive learning at one institute of Further Education, provides some excellent insights into how effective transitions are enabled and maintained especially if information on the students' needs can be accessed prior to starting a programme.

CASE STUDY 6.1: JANET – PLANNING FOR TRANSITION

Joe was studying at the local comprehensive school where he was predicted a clutch of GCSEs in the C–E range, including English and maths. He had a Statement of Educational Needs for behavioural, emotional and social difficulties. A Learning Disability Assessment (LDA) was created by Connexions and sent to the Additional Learning Support (ALS) Manager.

The LDA outlined that Joe needed his own personal space and could get upset if it was invaded. His barrier to learning was primarily his own attitude to specific subjects which he disliked and his short attention span. The Teaching Assistant was supporting Joe in class for 50 per cent of his timetable focusing on organisational skills and monitoring his behaviour, ensuring that he remained on task and kept calm.

The ALS Manager attended Joe's Annual Review in school where she was able to meet with him, his parents, his Teaching Assistant and the school SENCO. After lengthy discussion the ALS Manager recommended that, although his grades indicated the ability to achieve at Level 2, Joe's support needs would be better addressed if he enrolled on a Level 1 course where he would benefit from extensive in-class support. He would also benefit from an extra year to become accustomed to college life and build on his behavioural skills.

Consequently, he was interviewed and, in September, enrolled on a Level 1 course where he has settled well and is achieving good grades and feedback from his tutors. Joe is meeting with a Learning Mentor on an ad hoc basis to monitor his behaviour and work through any immediate crises. The in-class support will be gradually reduced over the year ensuring that Joe is functioning independently when he progresses to Level 2.

Subject

Section A: Student contact information

Student name	
Personal Tutor	
Email address	
Mobile phone number	
Parent/Guardian name	
Parent/Guardian contact number(s)	
Parent/Guardian contact email(s)	

Section B: Target grades

Alps score/grade	
Target grade	

(Continued)

No	Date due	Essay title/ speaking practice	Alps	Mark/ grade	Main action points

Teacher notes

Record of individual discussions with student, contact with Personal Tutors, Parents/ Guardians etc.	
Date	Summary of issue

Figure 6.1 Student record and progress card

Note: Alps reports are designed to give a fuller analysis on how students have performed in a given subject against national benchmarks.

Transition to Higher Education (HE)

Students in Further and Higher Education are not a homogeneous group. The British government's policies on widening access and increasing participation have meant that students in Higher Education comprise increasing numbers of adult returners rather than just 18 year olds. A body of research now provides us with rich descriptions of adult students' transitions to Higher Education, and of the differences in these experiences between traditional school leavers and adult returners. Drawing on the work of Conley (2005, 2007, 2008) that focuses on college (university) readiness, this takes as a starting point the assumption that, while providing support for first-year students remains essential, it is critical for universities to focus greater attention on what happens to students at school or college and how they experience the transition from school/college to university. Conley argues that there is a fundamental difference between being eligible for university, in terms of meeting admissions criteria, and being ready for the demands of university-level study (Conley 2008). This gap between school and university and between eligibility and readiness is the analytical focus of this and other chapters. Therefore in this section we plan, at the very least, to present how the cohorts of mixed age range students can also impact on the traditional school/college leaver's transition to Higher Education since our focus is on 14–19 age ranges. There is a vast body of literature on the first-year experience and on support needs of first-year students, yet much of this work takes as its main focus the first-year student once enrolled at the university. Measures of the extent of preparation for university study tend to focus on quantifiable academic performance such as UCAS points and grades. However, Conley (2008) draws attention to the need to understand the gap between being eligible for university study, and being ready to be successful at university. Conley's multidimensional model of readiness takes account of four facets: key cognitive strategies, key content, academic behaviours, and contextual skills (2008: 5). We begin the next section with Jacqui, who is a senior lecturer at a Higher Education provider, is a course leader for an undergraduate professional development degree and is involved in preparing students for transition from Further Education to Higher Education. The following case study explores her considerable involvement and emphasis on pre-sessional arrangements:

CASE STUDY 6.2: JACQUI – PRE-SESSIONAL PREPARATION FOR TRANSITION INTO HIGHER EDUCATION

The process begins at the recruitment stage where I am aware that choosing the appropriate course for the individual student is paramount and I begin the process by visiting local Further Education colleges in the autumn term prior to application. I arrange talks for students on eligible programmes and explain what the options available are and the entry requirements. There is also time built in to answer questions and give details of open events at the university and contact details for the students should they have further queries.

When students attend open events and express a more formal interest in the course, they are invited to join a social networking page, which contains information on the programme, activities to support students in their application and a place to ask further questions and speak to me if they need any extra support. Once accepted onto the programme they are given a pre-course handbook that explains the expectations of and support from the programme. Activities are provided, to encourage reflection on past experiences, understanding of how theory links to practice, key texts to develop personal philosophies and a gentle lead in to academic writing at Level 4. Students are also given guest access to the VLE and have a specially designed area to welcome them and encourage engagement in pre-course activities, discussion boards and generally to help them become familiar with the VLE so they are confident in navigating and using electronic resources before they begin the course. The VLE also enables them to have contact with a tutor to ask questions and receive a quick response from someone with the appropriate knowledge.

Jacqui has therefore emphasised the use of the VLE for effective pre-sessional preparation and transition.

The next case study is thematically linked in that it raises the effective and positive educational use of social media to create cohesive and prepared cohorts of students. Stu is a senior lecturer in sports coaching at a Higher Education institute in the UK and shares responsibility for the intake and induction of new students starting university.

Once the students are fully enrolled and on programme, it is vital that the programme itself has been prepared and validated with the students in mind especially in terms of induction, learning outcomes, and the first-year experience and student expectations. In the following sections we look carefully at the key points identified and suggest activities and ideas to enable effective transitions.

CASE STUDY 6.3: STU (1) – SOCIAL MEDIA TO AID TRANSITION INTO HIGHER EDUCATION

The growth in social media availability and use has allowed us as a course team to take advantage of the benefits of Facebook and Twitter in creating connections with potential and prospective students, during their transition into higher education. Setting up course accounts for both platforms has proven to be beneficial in a number of ways. In the first instance, we use social media as an information 'pushing' service that allows prospective students to get a feel for what is going on in the department as well as seeing course specific information to see what kind of projects and experiences they can get involved in. The flip side of this of course, is that prospective students have also taken the opportunity to get in touch with us to ask questions that have helped to ease their transition and induction into Higher Education, using a medium that is quick and familiar to them. Through social media we have had the opportunity to get to know students before they even walk through the door. The other beauty of using social media, of course, is that not only can we create student–tutor interactions, but we also see students getting to know each other before starting the course and friendships have already been formed, online, before the students arrive on their first day. For some students, having a familiar name or face around when everything else is so new, can really ease that transition and in some cases help to retain some students that might have felt a little lost and alone. None of this would be possible without adopting the use of social media on our course.

Programme and module learning outcomes

Writing module outcomes and then proposing a series of objectives to meet these outcomes that, in turn, are aligned with appropriate formative and summative assessment strategies to ensure learning comprise the essence of what a Higher Education programme is about. Yet if we adopt the formulas cited in 'The metaphor of scaffolding' (pp. 66–67) in preparing for teaching and learning then there is every chance of maximising the students' experiences for the better. Briefly a typical Higher Education programme is created by areas or departments and validated through official panels comprising Higher Education staff, subject specialists, external stakeholders and in some instances prospective students. The process is an attempt to ensure the relevance, currency and rigour of a programme of study. Once agreed and published, the ensuing programme and module handbooks become the focus of the lecturers' planning for learning and teaching. It is here that we can begin to plan effectively for each session. In the next sections we review and analyse the planning for learning for those lecturers who are involved in teaching students as they embark on a programme of study in Higher Education.

Level 4

What do we mean by Level 4-ness in academic work? Here is a typical list of attributes considered necessary and expected at this level:

Students should:

Develop a rigorous approach to the acquisition of a broad knowledge base; employ a range of specialised skills; evaluate information, using it to plan and develop investigative strategies and to determine solutions to a variety of unpredictable problems; and operate in a range of varied and specific contexts, taking responsibility for the nature and quality of outputs. In other words students should demonstrate a capacity for the interpretation and evaluation of knowledge, structured communication and coherent argument. This can be enabled if programme learning outcomes (PLOs) and module learning outcomes (MLOs) are aligned with the national level descriptors and subject benchmarks. MLOs and PLOs are described as 'Specific and concrete statements of what students are expected to learn' (Ramsden 2003) and what teachers should be helping them to achieve.

They are:

Derived from the Programme Aims and tested through validation processes and differentiated by level and presented under the headings of:

- Knowledge and Understanding (subject-specific);
- Intellectual Skills (generic cognitive skills including conceptualisation and critical thinking, problem solving, research and enquiry, synthesis and creativity, analysis and evaluation);
- Practical Skills (subject-specific and including professional skills and attributes with an employability focus);
- Transferable Skills (key generic skills of personal evaluation and development and interpersonal and communication skills, also with an employability focus).

In planning for transition at this level one might ask the following questions:

- Are the MLOs mapped to the PLOs such that every student will be able to achieve the latter?
- Are the module assessment strategies appropriate for testing the MLOs?
- Do we want students to pass every assessment task in a module? (This will require specific justification.)
- Do the marking criteria clearly differentiate levels of achievement beyond threshold?

Mapping of modules to programme learning outcomes at validation ensures that all PLOs can be met by every student – 'Higher education providers ensure that students have appropriate opportunities to show they have achieved the intended learning outcomes for the award of a qualification or credit' (UK Quality Code Chapter B6).

Anthony is currently head of academic quality and a learning and teaching fellow in a Higher Education provider. He graduated from the University of Oxford in 1978 and joined the BBC World Service, leaving in 1997 to enter the Further Education sector from where he joined a Higher Education provider as a senior lecturer in 1999. He is a former director and chair of the Northern Universities Consortium (NUCCAT) and former executive member of the Council of Validating Universities (CVU). He is currently an executive member of the Quality Strategy Network (QSN) and a QAA Reviewer and has been involved in several QAA Advisory Groups including the one associated with developing the new Part A of the UK Quality Code on 'Setting and Maintaining Academic Standards'. This considerable experience and his current position as head of quality have enabled a particularly insightful case study on the relationship between learning outcomes and progression/transition.

CASE STUDY 6.4: ANTHONY – USING LEARNING OUTCOMES FOR PROGRESSION

Learning outcomes, whether at module or programme level, are the principal means by which academic standards are set and achieved. National level descriptors and subject benchmark statements contained within Part A of the *UK Quality Code for Higher Education* are used together to frame programme learning outcomes that embrace subject knowledge and understanding as well as intellectual, practical (subject-specific) and transferable skills. The national credit frameworks, with their link to Notional Learning Hours, enable judgements to be made on the number and volume of learning outcomes, especially at module level. But it is the *language* in which learning outcomes are written and in particular, their transparency and alignment with assessment criteria and marking guides that are potentially powerful in supporting learner transitions. For example, an honours degree will typically define learning outcomes for each of its three levels to demonstrate to undergraduates the 'step-change' from Level 4 to 5, and 5 to 6. While the national descriptors are the main reference point for the writing of learning outcomes, alternative level descriptors such as SEECs, and learning taxonomies such as Bloom's, may help with conveying some of the subtler nuances. The challenge in writing effective learning outcomes is to use this guidance to frame outcomes that are clear and comprehensible to students and capable of being demonstrated through an appropriate assessment strategy. Reducing their writing to a mechanistic use of vocabulary, e.g. to 'analyse' at Level 5 or to 'critically evaluate' at Level 6, may satisfy a validation panel but is unlikely to be of much practical help to the learner. Because learning outcomes are written to align with the threshold standards, separate grading and classification criteria are used to measure performance beyond 'pass' level. Exceeding the threshold is naturally rewarded with higher marks although care is required to ensure that students who achieve 'only' at threshold level are not penalised.

As will be further discussed in chapter 7, 'Transition to Higher Education' (pp. 94–102), many new students arrive from a teacher-dependent culture and therefore cannot be expected to show independence and autonomy in learning from the outset. Therefore communication with all students is critical and effective inductions are crucial. Unfortunately induction is a catch-all term for so many things from tours to briefings, careers and welfare. Induction should be a process intrinsically tied to teaching and learning rather than a series of one-off events that precede teaching and learning sessions. Below are some approaches that can form the basis of effective induction and transition in school, FET or Higher Education.

Induction session activity ideas

We propose that the common characteristics of effective induction and transition activities:

- have a purpose and result;
- are relevant to your discipline, subject or vocational area;
- encourage group work that stretches and challenges but is not stressful;
- provide an opportunity for students to get to know other students;
- provide an opportunity for staff to get to know students and vice versa;
- provide students with feedback;
- are fun and engaging.

Some activities have specific academic purposes, that is, as academic diagnostic testing, which we cover in chapter 9 in more detail.

Discussing the demands, challenges and also excitement of the subject area during induction is very important. The importance of specific subject areas, which need to be addressed within the initial induction week has particular relevance if the points listed below have a subject specific focus. Possible subject focused topics include:

- What is study at Levels 1–7 about?
- Time commitment
- Attendance and punctuality
- What is expected of students?
- What can students expect from Higher Education?

A series of thematically relevant activities that can be carried out to provide effective inductions are suggested in the next sections and have been useful across all settings and transitions encountered in our research.

Activities around setting expectations in school, FET or Higher Education

Student expectations of teaching and learning

Small groups: By getting students to move into small groups, with people they know least or have never yet spoken to and by asking them to introduce themselves by name, they can draw up a list of their assumptions and expectations about education, their teachers or lecturers and other students. Suggest that they think, too, about how these assumptions and expectations may differ from other settings of which they have had experience.

Large groups: By sub-dividing students into smaller groups of people they have not yet spoken to or met they can be asked to brainstorm ideas onto the smart board or chart so everyone can read them, taking one from each group in turn. Students need not identify who made which point and by encouraging each person to contribute an item it can be ensured that everyone has an opportunity to speak. Then students could read out the idea from someone else in their group as it is often deemed easier by students to articulate another's comment in a new situation.

Function and use in transition: By using the brainstorm as a starting point for discussion and for addressing any misconceptions, it will be possible to make explicit any of the assumptions underlying academic life. Which teaching strategies are used and why? What are the students' responsibilities? The students may be used to a very different set of academic and vocational conventions, especially if they have studied overseas; for example, they may be used to being given credit for copying from texts, or they may be used to far more or far less contact with tutors. It may be helpful here, or later in the year, to move on to a consideration of attitudes to right answers (see chapter 10 for case studies on international and cultural differences) and what makes a 'good' student.

Helping students gel as a group

These activities are valuable when students begin a new course or programme of study and can be adapted depending on the size of the cohort.

1   Induction logs
     If students are encouraged to keep a log of their first week's academic information and to reflect upon it during one of the sessions some weeks later into the programme, it may then be possible to get them to reflect more deeply on these and learn how to improve their experience.
     Function and use in transition: If submitted electronically via a VLE, logs can give a good indicator to staff of individuals' IT and written literacy and they are a useful diagnostic assessment tool (see chapter 9, 'The Assessment Cycle'). Whether submitted or not it enables students to see the speed and journey they have travelled in just a few weeks. It could be used to get them to write a guide for future years, sharing what they wish they had known therefore making the task real and relevant and furthermore this could be used to induct new students in subsequent years perhaps as a Student Academic Mentor (SAM) (see pp. 81–82).
2   Compilation of fact sheets
     Students from the very start of any induction can be asked to work in groups that can be rotated and changed on a daily basis whereby they each compile a fact sheet of the most useful information they have found.
     Function and use in transition: Students could consider what has been of value and thus collate that material to help reinforce it in their minds, and begin group

socialisation. Also it could prove valuable to see by the end of the week what they consider of personal importance to them.

3 Interactive Q and A session

Students can draw up a list on a large sheet of paper of all their questions about the programme of study, the teachers and lecturers, study skills and other general ideas. The activity can be designed to run with staff providing answers or students researching answers in teams.

Small groups: Students can be asked to compile their lists and write their questions on post-it notes to stick them on a wall or board. To avoid shyness or concerns about reading out what they might think is a silly question, students can be informed beforehand that they won't be reading out their own, but an anonymous other's comments. All students can then be asked to put their questions on post-it notes in the centre of a table, move round two tables and read out the ones they end up near to.

Whole group: Students can be asked to collectively say whether each question is something they could find answers for themselves (from Programme Handbooks or Course Specifications perhaps), or whether it is something only an academic tutor could answer.

Function and use in transition: This activity enables staff to address students' concerns and worries right at the start of the programme and of course can be carried out in small and/or whole groups.

4 Common questions

Students can be asked to devise a list of questions that in your experience they tend to ask year after year. Organise students into teams of 4–5 people. Teams then compete to find as many of the answers to the questions as possible in literature that you provide from across the setting's support and academic services, noting exactly where it came from. It may also be a good idea to have back-up materials from other services to which they can refer. If practical and possible, encourage web searches on PCs or mobile devices.

Whole group: Teams can be instructed to report back the answers, saying where they found the information. All students can then be encouraged to look immediately at that source, where possible, so they have seen it for themselves. In the spirit of team building each should award themselves a point for every question answered correctly. At the end, attention can be drawn to how many questions students were able to answer between themselves. Any outstanding questions can then be answered or students directed to appropriate resources.

5 Personal skills and attributes for study

In groups students can begin exploring what they consider essential skills that they possess for the programme or course of study they are undertaking. These can be shared, and personal attributes like determination, resilience, patience, IT skills and abilities brought into consideration.

Function and use in transition: This activity provides particularly insightful opportunities to genuinely establish students' expectations of the level, programme, course and sector in which they are set to study.

6 The interview

By getting the students to pick a partner that they know the least about, they can get into pairs or groups of three and interview each other for about

5–10 minutes each. The interviewers are tasked with learning about their interviewee's likes about their programme, past jobs, family life, hobbies, favourite sport. After the interviews, each person should introduce their partner to the group. This exercise helps them learn about each other, and gain confidence in speaking publicly.

7   The introductory blog
Students blog 140 characters (Twitter feed length) about themselves on a VLE blog, including a picture. This can also be made more introductory by using blogs following interviews with the interviewer blogging about their interviewee. Using 140 characters means they have to be succinct and get the key facts in. This is also useful as a guide for staff to learn names and faces of students, and a valuable VLE induction.

Starting effective group work

We have researched and suggested strategies for effective group work previously (Bostock and Wood 2012: 115) that we consider pivotal in induction and transition. These are translated into the following series of practical activities that have yielded positive outcomes for students:

1   Suggesting ground rules
Individually: By asking students to make a quick list of things that they feel they should be able to expect from each other in taught sessions and in groups, and this could be a wish list for how they would like sessions to run. For some groups, it may help to give examples such as 'mobile phones switched off before you come in' or 'no interrupting when someone else is speaking'.
Whole group: Suggestions can be elicited, discussed and written up to constitute ground rules. The different ways in which people learn can be explored, and students asked to highlight what they see as the differences between this system and others they may have previously experienced. Consider this particularly in UTCs (see chapter 8 for further details) and other vocational settings.
Function and use in transition: To encourage consideration of essentials that may have been missed, such as confidentiality, respectful listening when others are speaking, punctuality, non-discriminatory language and behaviours and everybody taking responsibility for contributing. Tell the group that you will write this up for the following session so everyone has a copy. Also make clear that ground rules can be changed. Discuss how these will be monitored by the group; for example, will you or they draw attention to infringements? What are the penalties for breach? Encourage students to discuss this.

2   Personal development preparation and employability
Sharing in groups how they have worked in the past, what worked for them, what didn't, how they handled conflicts.
Function and use in transition: To develop sound and clear practices for group work whilst making students aware of the routes available to resolve cases of conflict or ineffective group activity.
    The ability to work effectively in a team is sought by most employers, becomes a necessity for most employees, and yet working well in groups is something many

students struggle to develop as a skill. Explaining the purpose of such work and its value is essential from the very start of every programme.

Group composition – self-selection or tutor selection? Random selection provides more opportunities, more challenges and mirrors more effectively the way in which students will be forced to work in the early stages of the careers for which they are being prepared. Free, online software can be utilised to assist, for example 'random student generator' programmes that automatically and at random can organise students into groups. It is important that students experience different approaches to working and learn how to manage their responses to those different approaches to achieve the best outcomes for themselves as individuals and for their group.

Introducing students to each other at the start helps develop their own support groups (see pp. 79–81 on how student groups can be helped to gel). However, we should generally avoid letting students select their own groups throughout their studies as we rarely get to select our working teams in the early stages of our employment, and so learning how to work with others, develop strategies and getting to know as many people as possible in our working environment is valuable.

During the first week, encouraging students into as many different groups as possible enables them to meet as many of their peers as possible in a 'working' environment. In subsequent stages of induction there needs to be an explicit recognition within at least one of the core units exploring the importance and value of group work.

Why we do group work is important in a subject specific context, providing recognition of the relevance of group work within the subject setting itself.

3   Student Academic Mentors (SAMs)
SAMs are students who are in the second, third or even fourth year of their study depending on the sector and setting who have been selected for their potential ability to help those in their first year of study. Arrange a visit from student academic mentors during the early part of the induction and set students the task of developing reports from those encounters specifically connected to the programme.
Function and use in transition: SAMs provide effective peer support to new starters as a critical friend and role model.

Helping students find their way around

1   Orientation activity: getting from A to B
By putting students into small groups and providing each group with a map they can be asked to find six specific areas within the institution/setting. They can film or take a photograph of each member of the group in a different location on a mobile device i.e. digital camera or smart phone and bring that back within a set time and/or collect an item from that location. On their return, students can then regroup according to the places in which they were filmed (or collected the item),

and explain how they got there, what they found of use in the location, and its value to their studies.

Function and use in transition: getting students familiar with the setting, layout and location of key areas such as the library and teaching rooms.

2 Acronyms

Task students to share acronyms from their past experiences, and ones they have already encountered in the institution/setting: FE, HE, VC, PVC, DVC, HESA, FTEs, UCAS, BTEC, NVQ, OCR, AQA, PT are some examples.

Function and use in transition: This activity helps introduce regularly used acronyms by getting students to recognise and explore use of acronyms and subject-specific terminology in all areas of their lives.

3 Quizzes

Subject area quizzes i.e. based on general knowledge, entertainment, subject matter and setting awareness all combined and tackled in teams. A quiz is a useful tool to reinforce essential information. It is a good opportunity for you to ask students to search out answers to all the questions they bring in the year and that you know they have in the handbook or elsewhere.

The quiz could be undertaken in pairs or small groups and it could be marked by the students. By emphasising that this is to help them, not to judge them, small prizes (e.g. chocolates, pens) can be awarded to encourage engagement. If possible it is worth noting who left gaps or picked up information incorrectly, as these are often students who get into difficulties later and it is one way in which students can be considered to be 'at risk'. Students able in many other aspects of study may not be adept at administrative practicalities and some may need extra guidance. Quizzes can also be composed by previous year groups, referencing what they felt was valuable to learn during induction.

4 Online and physical learning resources

This activity involves setting each group the task of taking a picture of a different library book from the reading list and bringing it back and emailing it across to staff and/or alternatively getting them to find a section in an online book and emailing that to staff.

Function and use in transition: The activity enables students to identify useful library resources for their subject, checks students' familiarity with the respective email system and provides programme teams with images to use on the VLE if required.

5 Icebreakers

People bingo is a popular icebreaker that is easy to customise for your subject group. Make bingo cards with areas to include a range of information from subject specific knowledge, generic information (locations: i.e. who's been to the library/computer suite), geographic (people from England, Scotland, Ireland, Wales, India and China depending on your intake), the middle child in a family, Scorpio etc. and group students in teams to complete the material.

6 Familiarisation

Examples of material and activities to familiarise students with the setting include:

- Guided Tours – especially those featuring shortcuts
- Quests
- Treasure Hunts

- Staff pictures and abbreviated staff CVs – don't forget to include support staff, subject librarians and other essential individuals who are part of the extended academic team
- Maps

Students can visit places compiling and sharing fact sheets of facilities on site, offices, open hours, and put this information on VLE as a reminder. Give students a list of items that they have to note from walls, desks or information boards at various locations around the campus. This might be the colour of the door, the name of key personnel, opening hours, and toilets – as long as it motivates them to wander around the setting and get a feel for where key offices and facilities are located. Include all the places that your students may need to visit at some point during the year, such as departmental/faculty offices, Students' Union, Careers Service, Learning Resources, photocopier facilities, IT rooms, lecture rooms, studio space, cafes etc. Finding awkwardly located rooms can help foster group bonding and develops a sense of direction. Of course it is important that such exercises are not unduly disruptive to the rest of the learning environment.

Addressing immediate concerns

Individually: Students could make a quick list of what concerns they have about the programme. This can be a particularly effective exercise to provide data for personal tutors.

Small group (about 6): Students can be asked to write concerns on a piece of paper, add to a pile and then each draw one at random to discuss together.

Whole group: One student from each group could contribute an anxiety that was raised, without mentioning who it was that had originally contributed this to the group. By circulating around the group more than once, a different student can be asked to respond each time. Responses can be presented as a mind map or long list and mind mapping freeware such as the examples listed below is extremely useful:

- Edraw Mind Map: Edraw Mind Map is a freeware mind mapping application with inbuilt templates and examples that make it very easy to use. Mind maps are easily conceptualised on computer and come with various embedded features like the smart drawing guide that makes drawing simple and supports big size and multiple page mind maps. It has inbuilt themes, effects and styles with automatic alignment and is compatible with MS Office.
- Open Mind: Open Mind is a freeware application for mind mapping and brainstorming that is finely designed to produce stylish and professional mind maps. It has almost everything required to diagrammatically represent thoughts or visualisations. You can make notes, use it for business or even personal purposes. It has features such as inbuilt effects, an easy drawing guide, themes and styles. This program is also useful when making flow charts.
- Blumind: Blumind is a brainstorming and mind mapping utility that is completely free. It can be customised according to user needs and has all those features that

are expected in a complete mind mapping software. It also supports chart layouts like tree diagrams, logic diagrams and organisational charts. It has preconfigured colour schemes and themes plus a simple interface that is useful for addressing diverse learning needs.

- Freeplane: Freeplane is a freeware mind mapping tool that is very flexible and open source. You can easily draw your visualisation and associated ideas with this programme's features. Once you learn its functionality, it will make mind mapping a fun tool to use for both educational and business purposes.
- ThoughtStack: ThoughtStack is a freeware mind mapping and brainstorming tool that enables easy diagrammatical organisation of thoughts. It has a simple interface and ideas can be organised in a tree structure formation that is then very easy to read out and edit. It has a built-in help file that explains almost everything required.

Whole group: Once the list is complete, students can be asked to reflect upon the list of anxieties. If they are surprised at how many other people had anxieties about starting the programme and how this makes them feel about their own anxieties they may actually be surprised and comforted to know most other people are also feeling vulnerable.

Small groups and then whole group: Students can be asked to suggest ways that they or others behave when they are feeling anxious or afraid in groups. By drawing attention to the fact that irritating and difficult behaviour in groups often derives from fear or avoidance tactics, it can be a useful endeavour for students to be aware of this, of how it can sabotage their learning, and of how it might affect their interactions with each other. Students could, therefore, try to approach their anxieties in a positive or problem-solving state of mind. Explain that this is something they will face in the future especially in new jobs and it is perfectly natural to feel anxious. However, the new setting offers the opportunity for them to learn how to tackle this natural emotion.

Function and use in transition: This activity enables students to share concerns, and recognise that they hold the answers to many of their worries, or at least have the knowledge of where to find the answers. It can also provide an opportunity to remind them that excitement and fear are closely linked and that they are not expected to already know the things that they are to learn, which constitutes a misunderstanding by many anxious students. Children can be delighted by puzzles, mazes and word games or 'fun' activities: addressing problems evokes a sense of curiosity, and as researchers, the development of that sense of curiosity is an essential part of education. Often, this fresh outlook and eagerness to take on challenges may tend to diminish particularly with mature students: they may be too afraid of failure. It is useful if students can bring some aspects of adventure, playfulness and inquisitiveness to any difficulties they encounter. This is done by encouraging students to turn their anxieties into challenges and to consider the range of resources, including each other, that may be open to them. These experiences and acquired skills will serve them well when they return to employment.

Solving problems

Solutions Focused activity

Small groups: If the list of anxieties, concerns and issues can be broken down into types of difficulty, each group can brainstorm ways in which each problem might be tackled.

Full group: Each person in the group can be asked to contribute one item from their list of possible solutions.

Individually: Students can write down the solutions they feel apply to their own situation. It can help if they do this in the form of an Action Plan, saying what they will do and by when.

Threes: Each student shares their action plan with two other people, who will undertake to check with them at a mutually agreed time whether they are sticking to their action plan.

Function and use in transition: This is useful in encouraging students to regard each other as a resource rather seeing the tutor as the answer to all their problems. It is also a good basis for building support groups later and for them to find some of the information on support services provided.

Case study based on master's research: integrating TEL

Jacqui and Stu provided some interesting insights around integrating TEL (technology-enhanced learning) into the learning environment or space in case studies 6.2 and 6.3. This case study, which is based on findings from research carried out on a master's programme, focused on the perceptions and behaviours of students who experienced TEL in their language programmes and is summarised into a series of points that constitute useful and innovative initiatives when planning for learning:

1 The use of TEL within the learning environment or space should be presented with other media, thereby providing many choices of learning method to the student. A student who chooses not to exploit the technology could access the same materials in another format and therefore not be excluded.
2 On-line materials should be inspected thoroughly for their suitability and adapted by teachers and lecturers to suit both their needs and those of the students. This could be carried out on staff development days and supported by TEL experts within the institution through demonstrations and presentations.
3 Learning environments or spaces should have suitable hardware available to support the successful integration of TEL.
4 Students' negative perceptions of TEL should be addressed through an initial process of induction to provide opportunities to experience the positive aspects of learning with TEL. This could be accessed via the learning resources centre, which provides tailor-made courses to promote such learning.
5 Lecturers and teachers would benefit from similar training but also from sharing good practice with other departments or institutions whose expertise could be

exploited through visits, hands-on training or even digital presentations showing the dynamics of teaching with TEL.

6   The creation of a TEL resource base for both tutors and students that could be accessed at work and at home and managed centrally could potentially alleviate the frustration of ploughing through reams of material on the internet. A well-presented and carefully focused intranet site would save on the time and energy needed to facilitate student learning.

(Bostock 2004)

Summary

This chapter has, through an understanding of trajectories into communities of practice, scaffolding, language and context, enabled an appreciation of the complexity of periods of transition. Using illustrative case studies from professionals who have engaged with students in transition, we have been able to present many ideas and strategies to focus on student expectations, orientation, teamwork and overcoming fear. In the next chapter we look closely at the roles expected of the teacher or lecturer during periods of transition.

Chapter 7

The role of the teacher in supporting transitions

This chapter considers the role of the teacher or lecturer in supporting transitions to ensure session content that is appropriately informed by the students as well as the teacher or lecturer. Creative and innovative approaches to teaching will be discussed and ways of using new and emerging technology will be explored. Practical hints and tips will be supplemented by real-life case studies from teachers in the sector. Students who are in transition are continually faced with new demands and new responsibilities in how to go about learning, and need to become independent in their self-discipline and self-organisation whilst acknowledging that learning (and its meaning to them) can significantly shift. Of course, this influences the role of the teacher or lecturer. For us this significance can be encapsulated in one quotation and in four succinct sentences:

> A teacher's prime task is to engage the student in the learning process. What the student does to learn is more important than what the teacher does to teach.
>
> (Minton 2005: 2)

1 Learning involves individual and co-construction of knowledge i.e. constructivism.
2 Learning may involve a variety of styles and preferences.
3 Teaching for Learning emphasises the role of the teacher as a 'guide'.
4 Learning is a product of active engagement, not passive transmission. It questions didacticism.

Teaching is creative and incorporates some self-directed learning. Correspondingly, according to Glasser (1988):

We learn . . .

10 per cent of what we read
20 per cent of what we hear
30 per cent of what we see
50 per cent of what we see and hear
70 per cent of what we discuss
80 per cent of what we experience
95 per cent of what we teach others.

The implication is that students need not only pay attention to subject matter or content, but also to the creative and self-directed processes of their learning. We accept that teaching and learning are inextricably linked and just as learning has its theoretical and practical underpinnings, teaching is also driven by codes of practice[2] and specialist standards that pervade each transition and setting. A brief overview will show how these are also thematically linked and are concerned with ensuring the best experience for students through best practice in teaching.

Historically Clark (1995), for example, has expressed deep respect for the learning environment or space as a fundamental context for teaching and learning, redefining the roles of the tutor to acknowledge this respect and stress the importance of sequentially meaningful learning experiences to create knowledge. The provision of sequentially meaningful activities through various media means that the tutor can guide the learning processes, and the learner can construct rules and models from the experiences. Vrasidas and McIsaac, for instance, argue that technology has the potential to support constructivist learning and can be used for active, authentic and cooperative activities (2001: 129). Interestingly, Vrasidas and McIsaac expand further on this claiming that the technology is not the deliverer of content but 'a tool which educators and students use to construct knowledge and store meaning creating multiple perspectives within a variety of contexts' (2001: 129). These historical yet pivotal appreciations have significant resonance in contemporary contexts that continue to shift and evolve.

Transition from school to college

As far as teachers and tutors who work with 14 to 16 year olds are concerned, the accreditation processes for those wishing to teach is vicariously overseen by the Institute for Learning (IFL), which confers the award of either ATLS (Associate Teacher) or QTLS (Qualified Teacher) on those who complete an approved programme of study along with a sound CPD record.[3] Alternatively, those teachers already employed in the school system should possess QTS for similar reasons. The IFL (2006) stated in its formative years that a realisation of such ambitious objectives could only be achieved if teachers were empowered with a sense of value within a professional framework that supports their initial training and recognises the importance of post-qualification development, be that subject specific, pedagogical, organisational or general interest. Consequently, all those who have qualified to teach since April 2011 are now able to teach in both the school and the college systems. There are three titles ascribed to these professionals: briefly, 'lecturer' is the designated term for any teaching staff employed in the post-16 sector. 'Teacher' is the term used traditionally in schools and is applied to those who possess a degree and teaching qualification. 'Trainer' is applied to those who possess work-based expertise that is passed on to trainees and these are found across the diverse settings associated with FET. Whatever the designation, a fundamental and pivotal role of each is to facilitate effective learning and to develop empathy for those who are struggling as well as those who excel in their work. In previous research we have shown how adopting either a cognitive or Socratic approach (see Bostock and Wood 2012: 47–51) can help support transitions for new students entering the college environment. If these approaches are combined, then our current observations and evaluations suggest a marked engagement of students with the subject matter whilst promoting autonomy and acknowledging and positively strengthening individuals' established habitual ways of going about learning. Conceptions of what studying and learning are about are usually deep-rooted and based on powerful experiences of school. The students, therefore, are in a good position to judge the appropriateness and value of any approaches to teaching and learning. We can show how a typical session might be planned to incorporate approaches that encourage structured group exercises.

We met Janet, head of inclusive learning in one institution of Further Education in case study 6.1 and in this next one Janet particularly emphasises how her team are able to directly support the role of the teacher involved in school to college student transition.

Transition through college

We met Cristina in chapter 6 when, in preparation for planning, she would always ensure a thorough knowledge of the students' abilities, progress and potential. In the next case study Cristina identifies how promoting differentiated activity and verbal communication skills is an essential and transferable element of her modern languages (MFL) programme.

CASE STUDY 7.1: JANET (2) – PLANNING FOR TRANSITION

Kathryn is a Learning Support Manager in a moderately sized Further Education college in a catchment area where a selection process takes place prior to the transfer to secondary education. The majority of secondary schools have a sixth form provision with the local grammar schools attracting the pupils with the highest ability. The Further Education college encourages applications from pupils with the full range of abilities and offers the usual variety of academic and vocational courses.

As an outcome of the disclosure of a learning need or disability on the application form, Kathryn becomes involved in the transition process from school to college. She works closely with Connexions and external agencies, such as the Sensory Impairment Service, to collate relevant information. She then attends the Annual Review meetings at the applicant's school providing timely and valuable information to support a smooth transition to college. Involvement at this stage also allows time for any reasonable adjustments to be put in place.

Kathryn then evaluates all the information obtained and makes recommendations for appropriate courses based on a holistic approach. For instance, the applicant's predicted grades may indicate that a Level 2 course would be achievable but the applicant's needs may be such that a Level 1 course, with support, would ensure retention, success and ultimate progression.

Following this, Kathryn compiles guidance notes for tutors, ensuring that the information is available from the student's first day at college in September. Finally, she is available from enrolment, through induction and throughout the year to provide advice to students, tutors and parents.

CASE STUDY 7.2: CRISTINA – IMPROVING FLUENCY IN SPEAKING (MFL LEVEL 3)

Speaking and giving opinions using advanced vocabulary is an essential part of the AS course of study. As a language teacher role play and pair work is a common activity. However, I wanted to use an activity that had an element of differentiation and encourage the students to speak without notes and reading. So, over the last few years I have been using 'speed dating activities' for speaking. The session usually starts with a grammar point (el subjunctuivo con expresiones como 'es importante que'); this is linked to a topic (las drogas y los jóvenes), with students working in pairs to write their own sentences to answer a set of questions related to a speaking card. Students can use their booklet and online dictionary in order to encourage independent thinking. Once this is completed I offer support to check that grammar and spelling are correct. Students are then moved to a pre-arranged set of tables for the speed dating activity. I usually use a youtube French or Spanish song to time the activity. Every time I stop the music the students have to move around and ask or answer the questions (depending which side of the table they are sitting). This activity works very well for differentiation, support and sharing. Students have the opportunity to practise their answer at different levels depending who they are paired with. The weaker students are able to learn from more advanced students, and all students are told on the last round to answer the questions without their notes. As a plenary I encourage my students to pick up one good grammatical construction that they have heard from another student.

Sarah is a FET lecturer, working in the Business and Marketing area with ten years of teaching experience and an active involvement in the development of all new teaching staff in her department. The area that she adds value to is the difficult transition for learners from a Level 2 to a Level 3 course, whether it be in the B/TEC or more traditional GCSE/GCE route. Using the metaphor of stepping stones, Sarah highlights the significance of developing higher order thinking skills as students transit through the initial stages of Level 3 study.

CASE STUDY 7.3: SARAH – DEVELOPING HIGHER ORDER THINKING SKILLS

Getting learners used to higher level critical evaluation skills that are necessary for a Level 3 qualification is always tricky. One particular fun way to develop that skill is what we refer to as the stepping stones method. At Level 2 students are used to giving the answer to questions without really justifying their answers. With the stepping stones method we try to teach that the journey to arriving at the answer is just as important as getting the answer in the first place. I have laminated several large stepping stones that you would find in streams to cross water. At one side of the class room is one stepping stone and the other side another stepping stone. They have to slowly work out and justify their answer stone by stone. It is a fun way to make them focus and explain in detail how they come up with some answers to problems. We often then consolidate their answers afterwards in a flow chart, again demonstrating and showing them how to order their thought process. We all do it in every area of our lives and we very quickly come to quite complex decisions, but slowing down the process and making students take one step at a time and explain each of the steps really lays the foundations for them to acquire and use effectively their own critical evaluation skills in all subject areas.

Nuria is also a modern languages tutor in FET who has worked in secondary education and currently works in an independent sixth form college.

CASE STUDY 7.4: NURIA – TRANSITION FROM HIGH SCHOOL TO SIXTH FORM 'HOMEWORK'

I find that year 12 students don't appreciate the importance of 'hitting the ground running' by starting work in a language from day one. The transition from High School to Sixth Form is often an overwhelming experience, not only in the way students approach their studies, but also in the way they learn. In September I say to my groups that in order to consolidate their learning they need to study little but often. In order to get them to do this my strategy is to set homework on a weekly basis. For example they do a listening exercise every week and have to submit it on Thursdays; the reading comprehension needs to be submitted on Fridays and the oral preparation is on the day they have the oral class.

Obviously other homework is also given according to the topic in hand and from session to session, for example grammar exercises and essay writing at the end of each topic. I found this an effective way to get students working little but often because they have to learn how to organise their time in order to prepare their homework to be on time. Also they get into the habit of looking at the subject regularly and practising different skills at the same time. As important as it is for the students to do the homework and present it on time, it is crucial that the teacher makes sure they have enough resources to complete. Resources should be topic related to make learning more effective and it should also be checked and corrected on the planned days and those students that don't do it should be challenged. I have found that the first weeks are the most demanding ones for the teacher but soon after the students start responding well and get used to their work load.

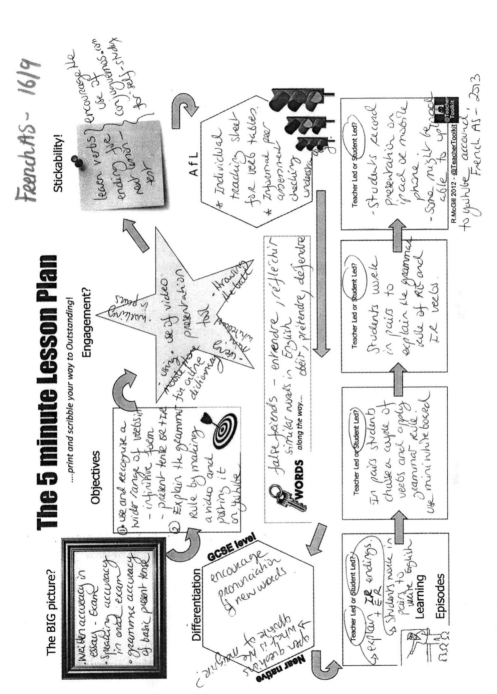

Figure 7.1 The 5-minute lesson plan

Transition to Higher Education (HE)

In 2012 *The Telegraph* (Paton 2012) reported on a survey carried out amongst researchers by Cambridge Assessment, which concluded 'Some six-in-10 academics are providing "additional support classes" for first year undergraduates because students are so poorly prepared for the demands of higher education'. In most cases, universities stage basic sessions in writing skills – particularly for students taking degrees in English – amid complaints that too many school-leavers struggle to structure an essay, spell properly or use correct grammar. This is somewhat one-sided and pessimistic and makes a much generalised assumption about pre-university teaching and learning. What is clear, however, is the shift in the perception of teaching and the student experience as of more importance than previously thought; that is, because of an increase in fees, NSS surveys and marketisation of Higher Education. In table 7.1 we provide an overview of the divide to perhaps provide insights into staff and student perceptions.

Indicator 5 of the UK Quality Code for Higher Education Chapter B4 (2013: 12) states that 'higher education providers put in place policies, practices and systems that facilitate successful transitions and academic progression'. Therefore lecturers and programme teams can work together to provide evidence of engagement with Undergraduate/Postgraduate Taught Degree Frameworks:

- department's strategy for student Induction and Transitions and its alignment with the respective guides to effective academic induction;
- department's retention strategy;
- strategy for academic and transferable skills development;
- personal tutor arrangements;
- Personal Development Planning (PDP);
- support for Joint Honours, part-time and distance learning students (where applicable);
- support for international students (where applicable);
- how inclusion and protected characteristics have been taken into account within curriculum development and student support.

In the next sections we will identify what we believe to be successful induction strategies preceded by an introductory case study that stresses the possibilities and potentials of social media in preparing for transitions. Stu, whom we met in case study 6.3, has focused his institutional fellowship on the integration of social media into teaching and learning, with a view to helping students to develop positive digital identities that will enhance employability throughout the programme of study and aid their transition into industry.

Strategic induction points or 'firsts' including the first week of study

In our experience we have found that the minimum requirements of an induction should be that every student finishes the first week of induction knowing:

- Rooms for classes, lectures or study, key areas and academic and support staff within the setting relevant to their programme or course of study.

Table 7.1 Nature of the divide between school/college and university teaching roles

Who is teaching (teacher identity)	What is taught (content of courses)	How teaching is delivered (pedagogy)	How students learn (pedagogy)	How the subject is presented (representation)	Where teaching and learning occurs (educational spaces)
Teacher as 'jack-of-all-trades'	Dated and restricted content imposed by curricula and associated textbooks	Restricted to rote learning or 'spoon-feeding'	Teacher-led (dependent/passive) learning. Amassing facts, describing	One view, one 'right' answer. Multiple views, partial representations, numerous answers	Restricted spaces: predominantly classrooms

Who is teaching (lecturer identity)	What is taught (content of courses)	How teaching is delivered (andragogy)	How students learn (andragogy)	How the subject is presented (representation)	Where teaching and learning occurs (educational spaces)
Research reactive, with breadth of knowledge. Lecturer as expert. Research-active with depth of knowledge	Current and diverse content emanating from a research base	Variety of means from cohort lectures to small group tutorials. Issues-based	Student-led (independent/active) learning	Critical and theoretical enquiry, exploration and discovery (heuristics[a]). Process-based	Varied spaces: lecture theatres, classrooms

[a] from *heuristikos* – the Greek word for 'discovery'.

CASE STUDY 7.5: STU (2) – USING SOCIAL MEDIA PLATFORMS TO SUPPORT TRANSITIONS

We are currently rolling out a course-wide integration of three social media platforms (Twitter, Youtube and Wordpress Blogs). The intentions behind this are two-fold. Initially, student engagement in these Web 2.0 platforms will hopefully allow us to develop broader discussion of subject content, not only within the context and boundaries of the course, but beyond the lecture hall and seminar rooms to a much wider, potentially national and international community. In addition to this, an integrated approach to using these tools throughout the course of their studies will allow students to develop and manage a positive online presence and create a digital footprint that can potentially enhance employability in a very competitive graduate job market. This online presence will act as a digital record of achievement that will track the development and transitions across their three years of study. Students will effectively be engaged in developing their very own online 'Brand You'. Whilst this project is in the very early stages, one thing we are noticing is that whilst students know of, use and understand the technologies prior to beginning the course, they are not using these platforms to engage in any kind of learning or development. This project should help us better understand the issues and concerns.

- Where to find and log in to the respective VLE and their student email accounts.
- What is expected of them as professional students in terms of attendance and behaviour i.e. learning contracts.
- What each student can expect from staff – academic and administration.
- An outline of the content, assessment types and value of their programme – online (they can print a copy if they need to).
- Where to find a computer and how to log in using the setting's network.
- Names and faces of ten of their peers.
- The work of Learning Services and Student Services and how to contact them.

Each essential 'first' should be clearly covered in a core module (which module is covering which should be decided by the programme team in their planning for the forthcoming year), although module leaders may wish to reinforce induction into each of these areas within each of their modules.

First taught session

Establish the requirements regarding mobile phones, laptops, lateness, different ways of taking notes, use of video cameras and recording equipment in sessions. This should set the scene at each of the different ways of learning in sessions – lectures, seminars, tutorials, practicals etc. so students understand what is expected of them, and how they can best use these ways of learning to enhance their knowledge. You may want to include note-taking, blogs etc.

First piece of academic writing

Introduce the principles of academic writing, explore what students have done in this area before (if anything), and look at how what is required in Higher Education is different from their previous experiences. This can also be an ideal place to introduce the concept and reality of plagiarism. A useful structure could be:

Academic writing:

- is made easier by prior planning;
- makes it clear how the question is to be addressed, the general direction and why;
- sets out the main ideas clearly;
- makes it clear how the main ideas relate to each other;
- takes the reader through answers in a logical, progressive way;
- helps the reader to remember what has been said;
- organises groups of related information in paragraphs;
- uses connecting words and phrases to relate each point/idea to earlier and later points.

First assessment

Explain the process, procedures, where to find and how to meet learning outcomes, grading criteria, pitfalls, and problems from previous student experiences.

First feedback

Explain how it comes, where it comes, what it is for, what students should do with it. Even if you do not have formal action plans for students to develop from their feedback to assist with future work, it is worth suggesting this can be a personal development strategy.

First grades

Students need to know what a grade means in terms of quality of work, the grading scale, what a pass means, what happens if there is a fail – can they instantly retake, what do grades that are provisional mean, when are grades provisional, how and when do students get their final agreed grade for a piece of work? etc.

To avoid information overload at the start of programmes introduce specific information at the times it is needed; for example, academic writing when introducing an assessment requiring an essay. Plagiarism and referencing go hand-in-hand with concrete examples as students are working towards their first assessment.

Many colleges, for instance, provide all their new students with free pen drives (or even free iPads!) with the information they need including blogs and podcasts of the key information. We have also recently researched the use of augmented reality platforms to enhance and incentivise the induction and transition phase with interactive multi-media. One innovative idea to support subject pedagogy would involve the use of *Aurasma*, which is an augmented reality platform created by the Autonomy Corporation. Primarily designed for 3G and 4G mobile devices, it uses the device's video camera to recognise pre-trained images and overlay an image or video so that the video tracks as the camera is moved. In this way, students can see digital videos of aspects of sessions they have enrolled on or that their teachers and lecturers have provided to produce a series of still images that by using Aurasma[4] can trigger a simulated digital video representation of the image in real time.

First six weeks

Minimum requirements for the first term/semester of induction are that every student has:

- undergone a diagnostic assessment (within the first month) and been offered additional support where necessary;
- been introduced to the work of Learning Services' Academic Support Division and explored subject-specific library resources around a learning activity within their programme (an information literacy session);
- met with their personal tutor either in a small group or individually;
- undergone individual diagnostic testing.

Typical areas and activities include:

Written English

Free writing longhand with a time limit of fifteen minutes and without the use of dictionaries or internet assistance. Topics such as: Why I chose this programme and Where I hope this programme will take me when I graduate? are valuable for programme teams, personal tutors and students to reflect upon in future years.

It may be useful to ask students to:

- include a plan for their writing
- present work with headings underlined
- present writing that is neat and legible or word-processed
- write sentences that are complete
- provide correctly punctuated work
- demonstrate an understanding of basic grammatical concepts
- underline any spellings which are problematic.

An example of this could be to choose one of the following statements and write at least ONE full page (Level 2 students) or ONE AND A HALF pages (Level 3 students) expressing criticality on the subjects of:

- drugs
- eating meat

- dangerous sports
- alcohol
- families
- smoking.

Once completed, possible activities to address any issues or concerns or indeed to build on a very good or excellent premise might be laid out in the following way:

Interpreting results: If there are significant grammatical, spelling or literacy issues, determine by reference to other diagnostic activities whether inadequate language skills or a learning difficulty appear evident.

Listening and comprehension

Students can be encouraged to discuss in groups or pairs for a set time their hopes or fears and then write a rapid report, each summing up what was said to cover all views they have heard.

Interpreting results: Slow recall and report writing may indicate a learning difficulty. Inability to hear may indicate a hearing impairment. A lack of balance in the report may be indicative of the need to develop analytical skills.

Oral English

The group can be directed to describe their journey to the setting in three short sentences.

Interpreting results: Hesitancy may indicate language difficulties or extreme nervousness.

IT skills

Students could undertake a task such as contributing to an introductory blog about themselves with an image and text about themselves or participate in a VLE discussion board question in their first week. They could support this by finding a particular subject website.

Interpreting results: Students struggling to access documents will benefit from additional support.

Numeracy

From the outset we feel we must make a clear distinction between the notions of qualifications i.e. GCSE Maths and being functionally numerate. The need for this will vary from subject to subject but interpretation of numerically presented material will be required in most programmes. Induction can build confidence with numbers and include reading charts and tables, extracting simple information perhaps by using positive data from your previous year's students' feedback questionnaires or programme statistics. Simple calculations from data sets including mean values, range and simple arithmetical processes are probably all that is required.

Interpreting results: Students exhibiting difficulties with numerical literacy may need additional support, possibly through their personal tutor. If significant numbers require support, then the department should consider making special arrangements for the group.

Acting on diagnostic evaluation

Language assistance – refer to additional learning support services.

Learning difficulties – refer students with disabilities to Inclusive Services or Student Services.

Specialist help for particular software/hardware introductions should be available within the relevant faculties or departments.

IT help and Computer Skills help – refer to Learning Services or specialists within your department.

Student expectations

For a range of reasons, students often enter their new place of study with a false or unclear set of impressions about what to expect. This is especially true for students who are the first generation of their family to enter Higher Education or who come from schools where Higher Education is not a common destination. Most students bring with them some notion of support and guidance from school or Further Education where numbers are smaller, study is more structured (see table 7.1), fewer teaching staff may be involved and where groups are small enough for everyone to know everybody else's name. They often have unrealistic expectations of the amount of pastoral care and study support that will be available at the institution/ setting. They can expect a 'school' atmosphere, with staff taking responsibility for their learning and attendance. For international students, there are also issues around adapting to a different country, culture and educational process. Often they will have experienced higher levels of staff/student contact and more didactic approaches to teaching.

There are clear implications for personal tutoring arrangements, including monitoring and support for part-time and distance learning students, opportunities for Personal Development Planning (PDP) and the development of academic and key transferable skills:

- updated induction programme ready online for the weekend before induction begins;
- many will prefer to access it via their laptop or smartphone;
- print copies can be made available on day 1 for those who forget it.

It can come as a great shock for students to find that they are expected to direct their own study outside contact time, and to manage most of their study problems for themselves. Many students have little notion of how to make use of undirected study time. They may not realise that they will be expected to hunt down information for themselves through reading, online resources, the internet or other means. They may assume it is the lecturer's job to feed them whatever information they need and may even be outraged at the amount they are expected to do for themselves. They may even expect that lecturers are there to do all the work of making sense of complex materials for them. It is not unusual to find students in Higher Education who have never read an academic book prior to entry and who are surprised that anyone should expect them to read one. On the other hand, there are also the students who expect to be reading the entire reading list within the first few weeks. Students may also have little idea of the difference between Further Education and Higher Education levels of study.

Supporting resilience

Students sometimes comment that they came to university in order to develop their writing or to improve their grammar as if that were their main goal, not grasping that this is far from the prime function of a university. Students who are confused about the essentials for survival on-programme will not pay sufficient attention to their studies. Some believe that they only need to turn up to pass, others that they don't need to turn up but can just study alone. They may feel that the sacrifices they are making in terms of time and money are sufficient to merit a degree. All these issues ought to be addressed prior to admission, but it is worth being clear in induction about mutual expectations, explaining why the skills that Higher Education develops are valued by employers and individuals. Students will need reassurance that they will be supported in developing these skills. So understanding students' expectations enables us to address them.

All academic staff have the opportunity to collaborate with student services to explore new and insightful ways to support students through peak periods of pressure and transition. The counselling services and the inclusion teams continually seek ways to work in partnership with academic staff to identify key 'hot spots' in advance and work together to address them. They share experiences, expertise and ideas as academics relating to peak periods of transition, whether it be settling in, returning in January to face assessment, the transition from one year to another, or any other period that can be identified, to ensure students don't fall through the net. Therefore we can begin to design new ways of working strategically together to support students through challenging and difficult transition points. Liz and Hazel both head up student services and counselling services in a Higher Education provider and in this next case study highlight their experiences of working alongside academic staff to identify key hot spots during transition.

CASE STUDY 7.6: LIZ AND HAZEL – AN INTEGRATED AND COLLABORATIVE MODEL OF PSYCHOLOGICAL SUPPORT TO ENHANCE TRANSITION THROUGH A PERIOD OF MANDATORY PROFESSIONAL TESTING

The university staff signpost students to counselling and support services on a regular basis when an issue is identified that is impacting upon their potential retention and success. However, the strength of this connection with support services, as well as the timing of it, may be crucial in maximising its effectiveness. As Egan and Cowan (1979) stated:

> If within an organisation, people are falling into the stream up-river and the counselling service finds they are pulling them out down-river, then there is a duty to go up river, find out what is happening and stop them falling in the first place.

At this university both academic and support staff were seeking a more collaborative approach and wanted to provide a stronger 'net', either to enable students to get out of difficulty as quickly as possible, or more importantly to pre-empt the fall and maintain the students' sense of achievement and confidence.

In view of this staff from the counselling and academic teams met to discuss and agree a plan together for a new type of support for students facing mandatory professional testing. In advance of providing the support the academic team 'normalised' the connection to the counselling service by flagging it in their course literature in relation to the forthcoming period of testing. They promoted the counselling service with an emphasis on seeking support in advance to maximise success, rather than promoting the service from a deficit perspective solely as a place to go when things go wrong.

The counselling service then consulted fully with the departmental team to plan a group session that would build confidence around testing and avoid individualising the problem. The result of the collaboration was the design of a bespoke workshop tailored to support students through this period. The workshop focused upon:

- Raising awareness of the influences of worry on anxiety levels
- Enhancing mental and physical wellbeing
- Enabling students to prepare an action plan to ensure mental and physical well-being for the test
- Enabling students to rehearse success and practise visualisation and relaxation.

Feedback from the students was positive indicating that they felt supported to take the test more confidently. Feedback from the staff involved indicated that the earlier intervention was more effective, more relevant and it promoted a closer and potentially stronger and more effective connection with the counselling service for their students.

Summary

This chapter has focused on the role of the teacher or lecturer during periods of transition and the case studies have presented useful ideas around communication, critical thinking, resilience and extra-curricular activity. Of particular interest was the instigation of strategic 'firsts' to ensure smoother and more supportive induction and transition opportunities. This was underpinned by an understanding of the perceptions of students' understanding of school/college and Higher Education teaching roles. The next chapter is thematically connected to the role of the teacher or lecturer but focuses further on the learning environment and the culture or ethos of learning in transition.

Chapter 8

Ensuring a learning culture

Developing students and ensuring learning takes place is central to all aspects of education. This chapter focuses on ways of ensuring learning is taking place, whilst developing independence and supporting students through transitional phases. Scaffolding approaches as discussed in chapter 6, the challenging of students to achieve beyond their expectations and the supporting of students with English as a second language are also considered. First impressions count and the way we communicate with our students influences their approach and relationship with their academic studies and the academic staff they encounter. Students learn from what we present to them, and how we present it, especially the style, inclusivity, information and accuracy. This includes emails, noticeboards, availability, personal tutors, presentations, and casual conversations. The sooner students feel part of the community the more likely they are to stay and the more likely they are to engage with their studies. Alienation, isolation and lack of friends are important factors in student withdrawal during the first few weeks, hence our covering of this phenomenon of ensuring strategic 'firsts' in chapter 7. Often friendships established within the first few weeks last an entire school/college/university lifetime. Group activities help students develop initial friendships, thereby setting a supportive but business-like environment for staff–student dialogue and giving clear boundaries and expectations. Again we suggested activities to support transitions in chapters 6 and 7. However, in the following sections we will consider five key points intrinsic to an effective learning culture (Active Learning, Motivation, Employability, Enrichment and Technology-Enhanced Learning) by concentrating on a new type of learning setting that has emerged and that we feel supports an ethos of lifelong learning for its students. Sessions are scaffolded and carefully facilitated to develop independent learning and they acknowledge the following prerequisites for effective learning:

- shifts in what teachers and students do in modern learning environments or spaces (passive versus active learning);
- constructivism and active learning in group and collaborative work;
- some key maxims for effective teaching;
- modelling, scaffolding and metacognition in learning environments' or spaces' practices and 'deeper learning';
- 'learning styles' and variety.

They prepare modern students for meaningful vocational and academic study whist also providing effective and supportive mechanisms for transition. Before we look closely at these new types of school, look at table 8.1 and carry out the following task:

TASK 8.1

As a group, draw a picture of a learning environment or space where a lot of effective learning is happening because the teaching is also effective. Write some labels on your picture to explain what good things are happening. Each group to share as a short one-minute presentation. Consider the complex common features from Lefrancois' exemplification.

Lefrancois (1994) has exemplified learning environments or spaces as complex yet possessing four common features:

1   Multidimensionality: i.e. possessing different personalities with diverse backgrounds.
2   Simultaneity: i.e. environments in which more than one thing is happening in a given time frame.
3   Immediacy: i.e. the requirement on behalf of the teacher or lecturer to give immediate attention to some activities in order keep a good pace and flow.
4   Unpredictability: i.e. a sophisticated amalgam of 1–3 in which some activity is accepted as unpredictable or unforeseeable.

Table 8.1 Passive versus active learning

Characteristic	Active learning or passive learning?
The teacher talks and the students listen quietly without talking	Teacher-directed and didactic or self-directed?
The students discuss the ideas from the narrative in a group	Rememberer and regurgitator or thinker and discoverer of knowledge?
The students copy out of a book	Note-taker and absorber or reflector and processor of knowledge?
The students find information on the internet and copy it	Regurgitator or constructor of knowledge?
The students write a list of important words they hear as they watch a short film	Low or high on processing activity?
The students copy a map from a book	Regurgitator or restructurer of knowledge?
The students find information on the internet about healthy food and write a poem and draw pictures about healthy eating and discuss them	Recalling or restructuring of knowledge?
The students put cities onto an empty map	Surface or deep learning?

You should now have begun to appreciate the advantages and disadvantages of passive vs. active learning and how within the multi-complexity of a learning environment or space inductive, student-centred activity can yield excellent outcomes for students. They are, in a nutshell, motivated by activity and we will discuss this in the next section.

Motivation, curriculum 14–16 and University Technical Colleges

In order to motivate ourselves we need to be able to visualise the outcome desired perhaps through extrinsic means – i.e. a qualification, promotion or money – or intrinsic means – i.e. an inner desire or passion to learn something new and meaningful; indeed a vocation. For some 14–16 year olds this has not been a possibility particularly for those in school who are labelled 'non-academic'. In recent years schools have worked closely with colleges of Further Education to give alternative curricula opportunities in hospitality and tourism, hairdressing and uniformed services programmes. However, this arrangement has been further developed and enhanced. The UTC is, despite its name, a new type of state school for 14–19 year olds of all abilities and is aimed at 14–19 year olds specialising in offering young people the opportunity to study qualifications leading to careers in the IT & Telecommunications, Business & Finance and Engineering Service sectors. They bring together local, national and multinational companies, the partner Higher Education provider and the college to provide young people with an exciting educational offer that will enable them to gain the very best academic qualifications but also to acquire the work-related qualities demanded by the business community. These partners will provide challenging and relevant work experience and there will be an emphasis on learning outside the learning environment or space and in real-life situations. Employers directly assist in designing the curriculum, delivering master classes, providing work placements and mentoring students. They are considered as an ongoing and developing learning opportunity to support the implementation of the government's reforms to 16–19 vocational qualifications. For example, preparations ahead of the introduction from September 2014 of Tech Levels, which provide students with training specific to a particular occupation, and Applied General Qualifications (AGQs), designed to prepare students for vocational Higher Education. Further areas include the implementation of the Technical Baccalaureate, including its potential impact on accountability measures for providers of 16–19 education, as well as alternative forms it might take. One interesting and innovative move within the current climate has also been the proposal to enable smoother and more informed school to college transition offering a broad curriculum alongside a specialist technical subject with a longer day than traditional school times (the day starts at 8.30 and finishes most days at 5.00) and a longer year (up to two weeks longer than most schools). It would allow for homework to be completed during the UTC day. Students spend 40 per cent of their time on the technical aspects of the curriculum. Not all of this time will be practical activity as it includes the theoretical aspects of the technical specialism. Table 8.2 shows a typical curriculum; however, students spend at least 30 per cent of their time engaged in practical activities associated with a particular specialism.

In the next case study Dave, a lecturer in engineering, discusses his role as a teacher in motivating students and maintaining an effective learning culture in a modern UTC:

CASE STUDY 8.1: DAVE – MOTIVATING STUDENTS

I suppose my response to the main desires of my students can be summed up as follows: It is all about establishing what type of teacher activity can impress and motivate students from the start. Not only do I strive to establish an atmosphere whereby effort and outstanding quality work is desired but also I try to establish myself as a great role model by being prepared, professional and happy in what I do. I avoid the demotivators of unchallenging or too challenging tasks by setting achievable tasks that involve appropriate effort. Cognitive approaches to task work are paramount so I endeavour to develop problem-solving skills to promote mutual and team respect including negotiated outcomes. Most of all I do not set myself up as a guru instead respectfully accept criticism and opinion from students where warranted. Yes I am a subject specialist and a professional but I also respect the students as equal in the learning and teaching process. To sum up, I put the students' needs first and I empower them to fully understand how effort and achievement brings success.

Employer challenges

A student's curriculum is planned holistically. Wherever possible the academic subjects relate to and reinforce the technical specialism. This activity is led through the project-based challenges set by UTC employer partners.

- All students learn about and use IT. The UTC has a clear strategy for teaching IT that is strongly influenced by the employer partners and a partner university.
- Business, Enterprise & Entrepreneurship.
- All students learn about business and enterprise through engagement with the UTC employers and entrepreneurs.
- Work placements.

Twenty days' employer led experience of work is typically a planned part of the curriculum and is overtly related to the students' academic and technical work. All students have the opportunity to work in a technical facility appropriate to their vocational study to offer opportunities to work on products to industry standard. The vision of UTCs is to give students an excellent academic and work related curriculum (see table 8.2). The curriculum is enriched by real work environments, equipped to industry standard and following high status academic GCSE and A-level qualifications, and professionally recognised programmes required by leading employers. They offer 14–19 year olds high status academic qualifications in addition to programmes in process engineering and environmental technologies. It is envisaged that students upon completion of their programme of study will have the very best academic qualifications and work-related qualities demanded by employers. Clear progression routes also offer opportunities into university and employment, which suggests an ethos of well-informed, lifelong learning.

Enrichment

UTC students participate in enrichment activities throughout the working week and where possible there is an international dimension involving exchange links with European and American high schools. There are Science, Technology, Engineering and Mathematics (STEM) challenges and contests such as Young Inventors, Formula 1 in schools, the Land Rover 4×4 Challenge and Engineering-Girl.

Opportunities for volunteering and community service are also prevalent:

- business and enterprise opportunities such as Young Enterprise
- Duke of Edinburgh Award Scheme
- community sports and leadership awards
- Youth Parliament
- a variety of recreational activities.

In conclusion, the essence of UTCs appears to be a capacity to provide educational experiences that empower the students particularly in their choices of study but more crucially by allowing well-informed transitions in a broader Further Education/ Higher Education interface. There certainly are challenges around the implementation of these reforms and new approaches to 14–19 education, including the timescale and resources needed to deliver the new qualifications. How well they will achieve the government's aim of matching vocational qualifications better with the needs of industry and higher education will be crucial.

Finally for this chapter we shall look at integrating technology into the learning environment or space to ensure a learning culture. We have consulted with two lecturers specifically who have experience of secondary, tertiary and Higher Education provision. The case study is written from a Higher Education perspective but is clearly useful for implementation across the transition phases. Dawne is an Assistant Head of Secondary Education at a leading Higher Education provider with responsibility for teaching, learning and assessment and student experience. She also holds a SOLSTICE Fellowship within the institution. Prior to undertaking this role Dawne was a senior lecturer in initial teacher training, specifically as course lead for the PGCE design and technology. Dawne has considerable experience of working across all age ranges and strives to plan for effective learning by clearly differentiating her teaching strategies used. David is a senior lecturer in design and technology education with specific responsibility for the BSc (Hons) course. He is also a member of several university groups including the Technology Enhanced Learning steering committee. Prior to working in Higher Education, David taught across the secondary age phase gaining experience in pastoral care and data analysis. In this next case study they offer insights into the use of technology in developing an effective learning experience.

Table 8.2 Typical UTC curricula

GCSEs	English (Language and Literature)	Mathematics	Physics	Chemistry	Biology	Geography	Electronics/Systems and Control	Applied Modern Language (German and Spanish)
Professional qualifications	Level 2 training in Food Safety and Hazard analysis and critical control points (HACCP)	Level 2 WAMITAB (Waste management qualification)	Level 2 Food Manufacturing Excellence qualifications (limited unit accreditation)	NVQ Level 2 – German and Spanish				
Technical qualifications	OCR Principal Learning in Engineering	OCR Level 2 Higher Project	Level 2 Performing Engineering Operations					
Themes and topics	Topic 1: The engineered world	Topic 2: Engineering design	Topic 3: Engineering applications of computers	Topic 4: Producing engineering solutions	Topic 5: Construct electronic and electrical systems	Topic 6: Manufacturing engineering	Topic 7: Maintenance Principal Learning – and overview	Topic 8: Innovation, enterprise and technological advancement

Theme A: The engineered world
Theme B: Discovering engineering technology
Theme C: Engineering the future

OCR = Oxford and Cambridge and RSA examinations.

CASE STUDY 8.2: DAWNE AND DAVID (1) – UTILISING TECHNOLOGY TO DEVELOP AN EFFECTIVE LEARNING CULTURE

In this study the lecturer creates a blog that is easy to do and completely free, explains David. Sharing the site address with the cohort encourages individuals to create their own blogs, and whilst the lecturer has access to each individual blog, the students can choose to share their sites with as few or as many of their cohort as they desire. Where a student chooses only to share their site with their lecturer, this is okay; and the lecturer can provide academic feedback and personal support to aid the student's development.

However, Dawne adds: when this method has been adopted, on each occasion without exception the cohort has chosen to create a shared learning community with each individual having access to each other's blog sites. This creates a private social media area, where students can create a personal portfolio of work, with viewers adding comments or re-blogging parts of another person's site. As work is undertaken the students post detail in the form of text, photographs, web links (particularly useful for research) and video. As work is posted, it is very easy to view an individual's progress, comment publicly online or privately in person on the work. Peers are able to do the same. Within this community students can see the progress and gauge the pace at which work across the cohort is developing, ideas, concepts can be shared and feedback can be provided as work develops and given when it is needed. The group quickly becomes a community and the impact of this strategy is greater cohort cohesion. Interestingly we observed a competitive element emerge with students comparing their progress with that of their peers, the overall attainment across the cohort when compared to previous groups undertaking the same module.

Summary

This chapter has looked at promoting independent learning especially in the early stages of transition and has acknowledged the super complexity and variety of learning spaces. A particular emphasis on the emergence of UTCs has also enabled a review of how learning institutions should not necessarily be streamlined into discrete primary, secondary and tertiary modes. Rather they should encompass an ethos of understanding where students have come from and what their future trajectories will be in an informed and nurturing manner. Underpinning this with e-pedagogy strategies can develop effective learning cultures.

Chapter 9

Integrating assessment for learning into the 14–19 classroom

This chapter considers assessment techniques that are appropriate for 14–19 year old students that maximise their opportunities to develop through self- and peer assessment. The use of e-assessment will also be explored alongside ways of embedding assessment for learning into creative and fun sessions. The principles of assessment *for* learning include:

- The provision of effective feedback to students.
- The active involvement of students in their own learning.
- Adjusting teaching to take account of the results of assessment.
- Recognition of the profound influence assessment has on the motivation and self-esteem of students, both of which are critical influences on learning.
- The need for students to be able to assess themselves and understand how to improve, therefore assessment introduces concepts of peer and self-assessment.

However, we must first consider a definition of assessment. According to Price *et al.* (2012: 9), and in a Higher Education context, definitions are so diverse and open to interpretation that the term itself could be considered 'redundant'. However, their own conceptualisation is one we support on two counts: one, they have encompassed terms such as formative and learning-oriented assessment and two, they have embedded within these processes a strong emphasis on feedback as a means to promote improved performance. Even the term feedback is open to interpretation and we concede that the nature of this will vary depending on the context and level in which the students are engaged. It must therefore reflect the multi-complexity of the contexts and levels that brings with it an array of problems. Since our contexts are threefold and based on transitions for 14–19 year olds, it is fitting to outline and review the concepts within a suitable heading in order to provide clear guidance to practitioners involved at each transition. We also feel that a focus on formative experiences and assessment strategies is more useful in developing successful students at all levels and transitions.

Transition from school to college

Whether at 14 or 16 (or indeed 17),[5] the transition from one environment to another can be a daunting one and as we have seen in earlier chapters, the pedagogies and

---

TASK 9.1

Do you think that the activities on the left can form useful assessment strategies too? Why? How?

Teaching and learning method	Formative assessment method
Discussion Game Quiz Role play Handouts	

---

approaches to assessment can vary tremendously. It is often assumed that students leaving school have been used to pedagogical approaches that indicate a distinctly passive, teacher-led curriculum base that, for the average college student, may have involved a degree of 'spoon feeding'. This teacher-dependent background does not have to be a barrier to effective transition nor should it be taken for granted that this is always the case. Involving clear and formative assessments that are student focused and which clearly point to how students can improve and succeed summatively can yield excellent outcomes for all concerned. First, we aim to show how practically any teaching and learning strategy or method can be transformed immediately into a formative tool that is beneficial.

Transition through college

Learning how to learn and using assessment to improve performance are crucial skills that students must employ as they transit through their college programmes. We shall now present some helpful thoughts and reflections on real practice at the front line about formative experiences and preparation for success in assessment. What are formative experiences? Formative experiences are about the deliberate teaching for understanding of what assessment is, what it is for, and how it works. This includes a significant focus on explaining and showing the use of Intended Learning Outcomes, criteria and ensuring students know and understand what feedback is all about. Working with real, meaningful examples, containing useful ideas and content in the discipline is the primary vehicle to achieve this. The best practice is to specify deliberate plans for formative experiences in the programme or module you design. You may present this as a grid or chart. Preparation for first year students, or those returning to study (or postgraduate) after a significant gap should be given particular attention. You could also consider this in the learning and teaching sections of any new module templates that have been included in the programme.

Unpacking 'formative' experiences prior to summative assessment

- All assessment can be considered to have formative elements if the very act of doing it is linked to developing one's application and integration of knowledge and ideas. This is particularly true if a student is building on feedback from the last assessments.
- This is even more formative if it is coupled with excellent, developmental feedback along the way achieved perhaps through discussion of plans, structures and drafts.
- Formative assessment is done in rehearsal and preparation for summative assessment ('it informs marks and classes') as it is a key element of the notion of assessment for learning e.g. having a go at an assessment and getting some feedback or an indicative mark to help you see how you are doing.
- Formative experiences are where the real added value to the student experience is at (and these can include formative assessments).
- Formative experiences are about deliberate teaching for understanding of what assessment is, what it is for and how it works. This includes focus on explaining and showing the use of learning outcomes and criteria and focus on what feedback is all about. Working with real, meaningful examples, with useful ideas and content in the discipline is the way forward.

Formative experiences through explanation and exemplification can include:

- Modelling, writing in front of students (showing and explaining how good writing works 'in action').
- Showing pieces of written work and describing their qualities (e.g. text projected up and annotated with comment bubbles and track changes).
- Marking it and explaining how the criteria work and writing the feedback one would give.
- Getting students to mark using criteria and to write feedback and talk about it.

Such approaches can be similar for all types of assessment, not just writing. So, in conclusion:

- Assessment is important as it measures student success. Formative preparation is important.
- If assessment is understood, students can be more successful.
- Formative experiences are important as they are more sophisticated than just getting feedback on a draft or a practice attempt.

In the next case study, Anna, who is a trainee teacher of Social Sciences – Criminology, Psychology & Sociology and works within a School Sixth Form and a Further Education College, discusses how she uses formative approaches to help students succeed in summative tasks particularly by employing useful verbs in student focused SMART targets. She teaches from Level 2 GCSE to Level 5 on Foundation Degrees.

Transition into and through Higher Education (HE)

Phil Race is a prolific writer of articles and papers on assessment and in his 'success for some what about the rest' paper from the mid-90s (Race 1995), he makes some prophetic and very salient points that we continue to acknowledge as excellent practice: Race stresses the importance of integrating the notion of what learners can do, when they go into assessment procedure, maintaining that experiential learning is not necessarily reflected in so-called 'good' qualifications. He acknowledges that successes should be devoid of discriminatory terminology and classification, asserting that the former ignores the true measurement of skill/ability and undermines real achievement. Despite the emergence of Records of Achievement (ROAs) and Portfolios of Evidence, the soft option of how good you look on paper is taken. It is proposed that progress be attained through a major overhaul of current assessment procedures, whereby learners become more closely involved in the processes, whereby attitudes to those processes are changed and relevance applied more widely to experience than outcome. Finally, the measurement of what is learned is questioned, the criteria and the divisive assessment procedure itself, highlighting a need for positive assessment rather than a narrow, inflexible and prescriptive regime that excludes the majority it purports to help. With this in mind and when commencing study, students should:

- have been told how to submit assessments;
- have been advised how feedback will be given;
- understand how to use feedback;

CASE STUDY 9.1: ANNA – PREPARING STUDENTS FOR EXAMINATIONS

When planning for my A-Level and AS-level Sociology groups I always ensure that I integrate assessments into the session that will prepare the learners for their transition into exams. The assessments involved within the sessions are always planned to incorporate the style of questions they will answer in the exam. I try to vary the way in which I carry out the assessments in session but ensure it stays relevant to the exam questions; for example, I will give a definition of a key word and ask them to write the word on a mini-marker board and hold it up (in the exam they would be asked to provide a definition for the key word). I feel that this is the most effective way of preparing the students for the transition into exams as they are able to apply the information learned within the learning environment or space to their answers. During the session I ensure that the students know how the content I am teaching is relevant to their exam and what they need to do to ensure they achieve the highest marks they can. For example I signpost my Power Points with AO1 (knowledge & understanding) and AO2 (analyse, interpret & evaluate) and discuss with the learners where the session content should be applied. I have found SMART targets particularly useful here using the student's action plan below:

Student's Action Plan/self-reflection	
SMART targets how to improve	**By when**
SMART targets	
Time bound	
achievable by the end of the training programme	
Relevant	
to the needs of the institution/learner	
Active	
use an active verb that implies change	
Measurable	
can be observed during the session	
Specific	
say exactly what the learner will be able to do	
Suggested verbs to use in SMART targets	
Improve	
Research	
Implement	
Answer	
Respond	
Set up	
Establish	
Investigate	
Maintain	
Review	
Complete	
Process	
Deliver	
Commission	
Update	
Plan	
Participate	
Demonstrate	
Resolve	

Signed (Teacher): _____

Signed (Student): _____

In other words this provides an effective and more strategic use of targets to enhance the students' formative experiences. The verbs help each student focus on each particular target and they offer clarity of purpose of outcomes.

- understand the essentials of effective academic practice (and how to avoid plagiarism);
- undertake a low weighted assessment activity within the first six weeks to familiarise themselves with assessment formats, submission processes, marking, feedback and return of work.

Formative teaching, learning and assessment can enrich day-to-day teaching situations, making learning deep and sustained.

Assessment preparation

Our analyses of data concerning why students withdraw from study indicate that assessment is a key factor. Not just because students are failed or referred but because the pressure of assessment can cause some to disengage. As stated in the previous section, students need to be fully prepared for how they are going to be assessed. This varies between subject areas but it is important to start students thinking about (and preparing for) assessment from the start of their studies. This can be done initially in a non-threatening formative manner before they face summative assessments. It is essential that we give students multiple opportunities to understand and experience how different types of assessment work at Higher Education level, such as computer-based, case studies and group projects. These form part of the learning process, and information learned in this way can be extremely powerful. The formative assessments can bring in the additional support so that they are fully equipped when facing the real thing. Genevieve, a senior lecturer and course leader in Higher Education, provides us with our next case study and demonstrates how she employs a number of useful questions which enable reflection on preparing students for formative experiences:

CASE STUDY 9.2: GENEVIEVE – EXPLORING FORMATIVE ASSESSMENT PROCESSES

We are exploring options for introducing formative assessment experiences for all incoming undergraduate students. Whilst this occurs in some curriculum/ programme areas, we do not currently offer or require that all students undertake a formative assessment to ascertain whether they have the skills for successful attainment. We are particularly interested in understanding more deeply the merits of introducing this form of assessment.

As a starter, some of the questions we have been considering include:

1 Should formative assessment be undertaken by all students or only those in particular curriculum areas?
2 Would it be appropriate for all students to take the same assessment or would this need to be tailored to the different requirements of different curriculum areas?

3   Would the assessments be optional or compulsory and if compulsory, how would we ensure all students had completed them?

4   Would it be viewed as a positive undertaking by potential students or something that might put them off i.e. more testing or a perception of this?

5   When would it be undertaken i.e. timeliness?

6   What expectations would be set for students who fell below a certain level? Would they be required to undertake further development activity?

7   Would these students be eligible for additional support, what form would this take and who would provide it?

Once decisions have been made, it is crucial that students and staff should have informed knowledge of the assessment cycle as depicted in task 9.2 in order to fully appreciate the benefit of each stage to them.

From this task you may have deduced the subtlety of difference between stages 3 and 4 as the former benefitting the teacher in terms of planning for learning and the latter as benefitting the students in terms of improving understanding and experience of assessments.

In their first case study in chapter 8, Dawne and David, both senior lecturers in initial teacher education, described how they utilised technology as a tool to help develop an effectual learning culture. The work describes a method of assessment whereby not only the tutor, but the peer group is able to provide almost instant

TASK 9.2: THE ASSESSMENT CYCLE

Complete the table below and give examples of each Stage/Type of assessment applicable to your setting and level:

1.   Explain the purpose of each stage of the assessment cycle
2.   Explain the benefits to the student
3.   Explain the benefits to the teacher or lecturer
4.   Discuss the subtle yet essential differences between informal and formative assessment

Stage/Type of assessment	Purpose of assessment	Benefits to the student	Benefits to the teacher
1. Initial			
2. Diagnostic			
3. Informal			
4. Formative			
5. Formal			
6. Summative			

feedback to individual trainees on their work, engaging the group in peer assessment activity and modelling effective best practice for these teachers in training.

In case study 9.3 they explain how the employment of a bespoke assessment strategy is used to support students' understanding of the increase in complexity required as they move between Level 4 and Level 5.

Frequently students consider 'assessment' to be a summative experience, where their work is graded at the end of a module. However, formative assessment is undertaken throughout; often via verbal feedback, draft marking and tutorials. In case study 9.4 Dawne and David articulate how the integration of a series of strategies for assessment helps students to understand their own feedback, but also seek to

CASE STUDY 9.3: DAWNE AND DAVID (2) – INTEGRATING ASSESSMENT TO SUPPORT TRANSITION

For students new to higher education, it is anticipated that they will be unsure of the academic difference in requirements of work undertaken previously, and as such strategies are put in place to support their transition that address both academic and pastoral needs. Having supported students well in their adjustment from further into higher education, the transition from Year 1 (Level 4) into Year 2 (Level 5) is frequently overlooked.

As Dawne explains: Supporting this transition is essential if individuals are to achieve their full potential in their second year of study, and be fully prepared for entry into the final year of their course. When they arrive an intensive series of support measures are in place to support students to bridge the gap between study at further and higher education, including study skills support, and preparation for academic writing workshops. Once an initial year has been completed quite often tutors assume students will seek out additional support if required, and students often believe no additional support is necessary. However, for many, additional support is necessary in order to make clear the increase in difficulty between Levels 4 and 5, and by highlighting strategies students can be effectually supported in order to make this next stage transition seamlessly. David continues: Immediately, right from a module's introduction, the marking criteria is shared, but building upon that during an initial session we require students to critically assess two pieces of work against the criteria. Of the pieces we provide one is Level 4 and thus would based upon their previous experience be sufficient to attain a pass. The other is Level 5, but of a low grade. Typically we have found that students award both pieces of work a pass, when in reality the Level 4 piece of work would require resubmission. Once this is explained, using group discussion and working under the guidance of the tutor, students are encouraged to revisit their initial assessments, unpicking how marks have been awarded. Quite quickly, through focused discourse and reflection they come to realise the difference and this we have found has been key in supporting students to make the successful transition from Level 4 to Level 5.

CASE STUDY 9.4: DAWNE AND DAVID (3) – ASSESSMENT STRATEGIES TO SUPPORT EFFECTUAL LEARNING

Teaching assessment to those studying to be teachers can be difficult, as it can be 'a dry topic' to cover theoretically, so the interjection of modelling practical strategies for assessment is one method adopted during sessions to support the development of knowledge and understanding, explains Dawne: You need to make it really clear to students when they are being given feedback that a verbal comment is feedback – but you need to make sure they know it is.

She continues: There are many techniques and one I frequently use is to ask the group at the start of a session how confident they feel about the task you are all about to cover. I have a 'washing line' stretched from one side of the room to the other, with one side of the line being not very confident and the other very confident and then I ask the students to place a note onto the line to indicate how confident they feel. This also helps you as a tutor to gauge the level of your 'audience' and adapt your session accordingly. Having completed the session you can then ask the students during your plenary to move their note, indicating how much progress they believe they have made, which shows visually if they perceive they have developed their understanding of the topic. At this point I often ask them to jot down any questions that remain – that I can cover at the session's end - and indicate I will cover these at the start of the next session or indeed I may decide to set the questions as an activity, for the group to discover the answers for the following session.

illustrate how, through modelling assessment in practice, trainee teachers can build a tool kit of assessment techniques for use in their own developing classroom practice.

Finally, in the case study 9.5, Dawne and David explain how, in the early stages of a new course, the use of interactive assessment techniques allowing continuous and immediate feedback to be received during lectures has proven to be extremely effectual in aiding tutors to gauge the pace and content of a lecture as it is being delivered, giving them the ability to adapt or revisit content that perhaps has not been fully understood before they move on to address a new concept or topic.

How to make your feedback work and preparing students to receive feedback

Indeed the last points are particularly salient and give us points to consider around feedback: Students need an appreciation of assessment's relationship to learning otherwise it is not worth doing. Where there is a greater sense of the holistic programme, students are more likely to achieve the learning outcomes than students

CASE STUDY 9.5: DAWNE AND DAVID (4) – INTERACTIVE ASSESSMENT TECHNIQUES

It can be quite daunting to ask questions when you are among people you don't know, explains Dawne, and this is exactly the situation students new to Higher Education find themselves in for the early months of study, which of course also coincides with a time when perhaps they are already feeling vulnerable.

Where students do not wish to make themselves stand out as being the only person in a group who doesn't understand a new concept, it can be difficult for the tutor to ascertain how effective their sessions are.

David continues: There are systems which can be purchased commercially that work in parallel with smart boards, or where these are not available the tutor can set up a blog or private social media area. There is even a system that enables students to text comments to the tutor as they are delivering the session. Students can text questions, thoughts or comments which enables the tutor to address issues as they arise, or group comments and questions accordingly, to answer or revisit during the session. By grouping questions the tutor can make clear that the same question has been posed several times and in doing so build confidence within individuals early on, and as a tutor be able to recap on key areas to ensure concepts are embedded thoroughly before moving on.

Another simple yet effective strategy tutors can use to gather feedback is via 'Show and tell boards' that are quite popular in schools. This is a simple strategy where individuals are provided with a mini white board and ideally when used in school, when the teacher asks a question, the children are required to write or draw their answer, holding it up for the teacher to view, enabling everyone to answer a question posed rather than one person at a time. This is an excellent way for the teacher to ascertain the level of understanding across a group, but also to help them to identify the individual levels of understanding. In higher education these boards can be adopted to perform a similar function, or as we have found they have proven to be extremely useful in giving students 'a voice', enabling them to give feedback on a session as it is being delivered.

on programmes with a more fragmented sense of the programme (Haynes and Kaholokula 2007). It is good to explain to students where the module and its assessment fit and why it is important in the overall scheme of things.

Derek is a lecturer in Art and Design and has amassed a great deal of experience in giving feedback in many formats:

CASE STUDY 9.6: DEREK – ALIGNING EXPECTATIONS

It is important to align the students' expectations with yours by explaining the purpose of feedback. I find that when students experience me marking, assessing and thinking out loud with examples of work on a screen, this empowers them more in terms of ownership. I often use previously marked assignments to show how feedback was used to improve the quality of later submissions. Other methods and approaches include asking students to submit brief evaluations of their work along with their assignments and letting them have a go at assessing pieces of work against the criteria, awarding marks, writing feedback and discussing the process. My approaches focus on reducing emphasis on written feedback because some skills, literacies and conceptual understandings are 'slowly learnt' and need rehearsal throughout a programme (Yorke 2001). Therefore it is helpful to practise with examples of all modes of assessment to demystify their purpose. As Price *et al.* affirm (2010), it is dialogue that supports understanding and engagement i.e. looking at examples of work and feedback and discussing how it all joins up. For instance, student engagement is enhanced if written feedback is supplemented with dialogue such as in-class discussions of exemplars and peer review discussions or discussion of feedback.

Joanne, who is a lecturer in Accountancy and Business Administration, provides further insights into feedback. For her a key issue in feedback is that students often do not understand what a better piece of work actually is and when students do not understand what is being asked of them this can hinder transition:

CASE STUDY, 9.7: JOANNE – PROVIDING FEEDBACK TO IMPROVE FUTURE SUBMISSIONS

In my opinion, setting students assignments as soon as they arrive at university could help cut dropout rates and integrate students into university life as quickly as possible. This involves making them aware of the quality and quantity of work expected from them as many probably need more structure in the first year. I have several approaches that work for me; for example, considering early writing as a diagnostic tool, clearly communicating the process, demands, structure, functions and timing of assessment and giving generic feedback to a whole group as soon as a general picture emerges of the quality of assignments. They also need to get the best out of feedback and preparation for this is also crucial. I always seek to clarify expectations and be clear what feedback is for and what the students' responsibilities are in terms of getting something from it. I show them examples and engender good study habits by diagnosing areas of individual difficulty and promoting engagement. Above all I feel it is important to let students see how it all works because when there are no secrets or mysteries surrounding it, they get it and in my experience perform better. For example, students can use feedback to think about what has been done well and what can be improved, to plan subsequent pieces of work, to prepare work in other modules, to develop subject knowledge and to prepare for personal tutorials. Students need to find out what sort of feedback they will receive: written, verbal or online and who will give feedback and when.

Understanding feedback

Points to consider:

- Students need to understand the assessment standards and criteria to be able to self-evaluate their work in the act of production itself (Sadler 1987).
- They need a conceptual understanding of assessment (i.e. understanding of the basic principles of valid assessment and feedback practice, including the terminology used).
- Understanding of the nature, meaning and level of assessment criteria and standards is important. In other words, seeing examples lets students into the 'secret'.

For example, students should be actively encouraged to read or listen carefully to feedback and how it applies to their work or ideas and how it relates to the assessment criteria. They should expect and be expected to ask for any clarification as they cannot proceed and use feedback they don't understand.

Summary

This chapter has reviewed and explored formative experiences and preparation for student success in assessment. The ability to make informed judgements on the work is a key graduate attribute (Boud 2009). Learning effectiveness (and student engagement) is strongly influenced by opportunity to apply feedback to future performance. This relies on:

- ability to understand feedback (legibility and interpretation);
- expectations of how feedback will be used;
- perception of self-efficacy – do the students understand enough to know they can do even better?

By using SMART targets with specific verbs and opportunities to explain the purpose of formative assessment in an assessment cycle, students are able to align their expectations with those of the teachers and lecturers and the programmes of study, use their feedback productively and build positively on their work to self-improve.

Chapter 10

Final thoughts

This chapter includes a review of some approaches to managing transitions and their impact on teaching and learning. For all groups of students, whatever their journey, recognition by all of the abilities and skills they bring with them, combined with developing clear understanding of the programme or element of the programme they are embarking upon, will go a long way to resolving concerns at an early stage. Indeed students are all embarking on a journey or trajectory, whatever their starting point. Activities assisting reflection upon their existing skills and abilities will reinforce their confidence to move on to the next stage of their academic development. These skills may also be 'transferable' from one context to another, from everyday life or employment into higher education, for example, so it can be extremely useful to set out an approach to skills development and highlight why there is an emphasis on skills development alongside traditional academic development. What is meant by transferable skills and how these skills are developed can be identified throughout a programme of study. Crucially there is a need to focus on transferable skills and employability in both vocational and academic specialisms to motivate various student types who otherwise might not engage, recognising that some of these will, of course, have different needs at different times. For instance, students from non-traditional backgrounds often start school/college/university with little self-confidence. This needs boosting to show them that they can achieve. So let us now consider and reflect on the various student types encountered in transition with a final look at supporting transitions at 14/16 and consideration of preparing various student types for transitions at 18/19.

Returning students

The needs of returning students can be forgotten amongst the demands of coping with new intakes. Many returning second or third year students express a desire themselves for clear, focused induction into their new year of study that we covered extensively in chapters 6 and 7. Most students may want advice on, or to change, choices made so you may want to consider highlighting:

- the specific demands of the forthcoming year;
- any new staff members;
- new facilities/ways of working using VLE, new learning areas etc.;
- work-based learning options;

- career choice and any professional body requirements;
- project or Dissertation requirements (an information literacy session may be appropriate).

New joiners at different stages and different start times

Within this group you may also have students who are transferring in from elsewhere or after completion of other programmes e.g. multiple start time arrangements, FDs and HNDs. You will need to consider the nature of any induction programme geared to meeting their needs. The activities we identified in earlier chapters could prove useful in creating induction and transition programmes at different times during the year. Some programmes have large numbers of students entering directly into different levels, for others the numbers are small; whatever the position on your programme, have strategies to deal with such direct entrants. Whilst it can be difficult to run a full programme of induction for mid-year starters you may need to run a similar or more condensed induction. Smaller numbers mean that the process can be more personalised if not as detailed. Some programmes offer a single session for these students in addition to the general inductions whilst others absorb them and their queries through activity-based sessions into the main student body from the start. Your subject and the number of such students should dictate how you wish to approach their induction but again, the earlier their specific needs can be met, the more likely it is they will feel supported in their transitions.

Students from partner institutions

Some departments encompass awards run in collaborative institutions either at home or overseas. If possible arrange a visit for students from the partner institution to the institution/setting and your department early on and at various stages during their programme. Ensure that students in partner institutions are aware of their rights of access to facilities and, wherever possible, make it easy for them to gain this access.

International students

It has been argued that there are many transitional needs of international students while adapting to a new higher education environment such as practical, emotional, sociocultural, academic, and needs around assessment, curriculum and performance. International students therefore may need to receive a separate orientation the week before general induction processes. As a strategic 'first' (see chapter seven, section 7.9) make arrangements to greet your overseas students and ensure they understand the need to attend the academic induction and explain its purpose. If you are expecting students from a particular country then you may wish to consider delivering some of your key documents (or even just a greeting) printed in their language. Some overseas students cannot make it in time for their induction week so if you expect large numbers of overseas students consider arranging a mini-induction for late arrivals (Hyde 2012). Hyde offers a frank and honest guide for international students, in particular a full chapter on the roles and responsibilities of the tutor and international student as well as an understanding of Further Education and Higher

CASE STUDY 10.1: TONY – CULTURAL AND LINGUISTIC ADAPTATION

Planning for transition from an international perspective is quite a multifaceted endeavour. There are many factors in place such as curriculum, culture, expectations and perception being the main ones. Expatriates worry about placing their child in a new school/college at the best of times, but the additional transition between settings adds another dimension. This is in addition to the curricular changes that occur.

For example, students go from an environment where they stay with one teacher and do not leave the learning environment or space except for electives. A student might only have three different teachers, one for the core subjects and one or two others for art, music, or physical education. This is contrasted with most middle schools where students must move classrooms. Instead of having one teacher for their core subjects, students now have up to four different teachers in addition to more subjects. It is not unheard of for secondary students to have up to eight different teachers.

This transition is sometimes made easier in some cases where students have had different instructors and classrooms for their electives. But in smaller schools/colleges with fewer class options, a student may have only been exposed to two teachers. Thus, they find it very difficult to adjust to more teachers, moving classrooms, in addition to the more rigorous curricular demands. Transition can be made even more difficult when expatriate students transfer into International schools where English is not the first language. This adds a linguistic and cultural dimension that can make the transition even more challenging.

Education contexts from their perspective. International students can feel marginalised if they are taught alongside full-time undergraduates, particularly if their numbers are small. It can be helpful to ensure they are introduced to each other and can form their own self-help groups. Finding a slot within your induction programme to specifically deal with international issues can help students recognise we see them as being part of the wider student body. Our final case studies 10.1 above and 10.2 and 10.3 overleaf are provided first by Tony, who is Head of Information Technology in an international school in Qatar, and from his perspective, he is able to comment on transitional issues that we feel have resonance across all levels as well as UK-based settings.

The next two case studies build on this challenge. Keith, who is director of studies in a University Business School, asks the question: Can students coming onto programmes in another culture adapt sufficiently to prosper? In excess of a quarter of a million overseas students came into the United Kingdom in 2012 and the majority of these students will have begun to adapt to their new surroundings and programmes of study. The issue of adapting to a new culture and environment will add to the initial feelings of uncertainty. However, the question regarding the adaptation requirement is the same when students go to a situation where a United Kingdom programme is run via an overseas partnership in another part of the world. Some interviews were held with students in China and Singapore studying on UK managed programmes run by two British university partner institutions. The objective was to measure the success of the adaptation to a new way of learning.

CASE STUDY 10.2: KEITH (1) – ADAPTING TO NEW IDEAS ON PEDAGOGY

The respondent is a part-time student from China on an undergraduate 'top-up' degree programme in Singapore. The student joined the programme with a Higher Education Diploma and began his studies on the final year of a BSc programme as someone in his mid-twenties who was working full-time in a Singaporean organisation. He admitted that he initially found the change from his studies at a Chinese institution 'very different' and at first a little awkward and not simply because of his relocation to Singapore. This was also because he was adapting to the use of academic language and a different approach to learning without the pedagogic direction that he previously found in his home country. The lack of the familiar prescriptive and the new unfamiliar constructivist approach was something of a challenge. He felt 'real concern' when submitting his first assignment having come from a learning system which was exam-focused. For the respondent said that he knew that he had adapted well when he used techniques from a module of study to solve a workplace problem. That was of benefit because problem resolution was recognised by his company and his position at work improved. For him that reinforced the benefit of a constructivist approach to learning.

CASE STUDY 10.3: KEITH (2) – BECOMING AN AUTONOMOUS LEARNER

Respondent two is a full-time student on a Higher Education Diploma in China. She has moved from another part of China to study at the university that offers the Diploma via a partnership with a UK university. Teachers on the programme are mainly British, Australian and Chinese but the programme is taught in English. Respondent two was in her second year at the university and said that she had found the initial approach to learning difficult but that the real difficulty was in becoming independent in everyday living. Her initial approach to learning was to cope with what happened in class by doing exactly as she was told or advised whilst wrestling with the changes in her everyday life. Her view was that having adapted to a more independent form of living and learning she was comfortable with both. Her progress on the course thus far has in her words been 'quite good' and she felt a sense of strong personal development.

Keith also provides some excellent theoretical standpoints to strengthen his research ideas presented in his two case studies.

Traditional views of Chinese learners have questioned their ability, as a group, to adapt easily and in some cases even succeed in a UK or Westernised learning environment. Ryan (2013) relates how Chinese learners are frequently viewed as being different in their approach to learning and notes how some Western academics might view them using a deficit model i.e. considering what the Chinese learner cannot do, rather than what they can do. Academics may identify what the students lack in comparison to supposed Western exemplars of academic virtue. Dunn and Wallace (2004) noted that Chinese students are accused of producing writing that simply reproduces published literature without critical or independent thinking, sometimes to the extent of being accused of malpractice.

However, Volet (1999) presents evidence that this viewpoint was, at least in Australia, found to be something of a misconception. She relates some work by key researchers (e.g. Barker *et al.* 1991) that counters this view. The studies reflect a tacit assumption that learning regimes in Western universities are the norm. Provided there was no language deficiency, Asian students in Australia performed better than local students. With regard to the case study respondents from Singapore and China, they appear to have successfully adapted to a Westernised, UK-managed style of learning. Saravanamuthu and Tinker (2008) note what appears to be a paradoxical issue, namely, Chinese students can appear to use rote memorisation that is often considered to be a surface approach to learning but they can attain high levels of achievement which in turn is considered to require a deep approach to learning. The nature of memorisation for Chinese learners has been further theorised as more complex than initially thought by Sachs and Chan (2003).

Ryan (2013) relates how in her view what she refers to as 'the Chinese learner' relies on assumptions that are both outmoded and outdated. The views are based on entrenched stereotypical notions that are the misguided premise of some academic members of staff. Ryan (2013) refers to a number of academic writers such as Junxia Hou *et al.* (2011) who determined in research carried out at the University of Northumbria that in effect the gap between student expectation and actual experience was narrowing. Also discovered was the fact that the gap in academic norms in the UK and China was becoming less pronounced and was in fact less of an issue than the students and their lecturers contended. Ryan (2013: 46) relates how there are, in her words, 'Many examples of innovative pedagogy being introduced in universities across China' that will of course help with adaptation onto UK or Western programmes. This re-positioning of Chinese programmes and, in the long term, pedagogy may help students adapt more easily to the Western way of learning, thus extending the success of students like the two case study respondents.

Mature students

Finally, mature students bring a wide range of experiences and abilities to their programmes and to the student body. They may be new to higher education or experienced students returning to study and can feel isolated amid large cohorts of school leavers. They can also feel patronised if apparently being singled out for particular attention. Ensuring that they are fully included within groups of part-time and full-time students from the start is a must. We have found that discussion and debate around the following points helps prepare for mature students in transition:

- current perceptions of the value of part-time and mature study in the context of increased tuition fees;
- funding arrangements available for part-time study and the confusion surrounding new student loans;
- improving the student experience of part-time and mature students, including the accessibility of student services; and
- steps to increase take-up and retention rates of part-time and mature students.

Summary

This chapter has focused on the diverse student body and has provided a review with illustrative case studies which emphasise the necessity for dialogue and discussion amongst curriculum teams when planning for transition. We do feel, however, that there are still further areas to focus on and develop, for example:

- Challenges around delivering new qualifications, including resources, teacher training, and the proposed time frame;
- How well the reforms encourage and prepare students to continue into vocational learning or professional training; and
- The implementation of the technical baccalaureate and possible alternative forms it could take.

These are of course very much our aims for the future where we will continue to look at new and innovative ways of developing these further and their implications for the learning environments or spaces of the future. In particular we intend to further our research into learner empowerment and decolonising pedagogies that we feel will promote and sustain multicultural approaches to teaching and learning.

> Traditional in structure, the humpback bridge survives because the volume of traffic wanting to cross is not sufficient to generate demands for change to a more efficient form of bridge. Its narrowness restricts passage to certain categories of road users. Unable to see over it, one forms a view of what is going on at the other side by listening to reports brought back or by making surmises from those activities that create sufficient noise, unless one is prepared to venture across oneself.
>
> (Steed and Sudworth 1985: 23)

Although this analogy of a humpback bridge was first used 25 years ago by Steed and Sudworth in the context of the transition from primary to secondary school, this metaphor remains richly descriptive of the transition from school or college to university depicted in these chapters. For most students, an outdated and inefficient humpback bridge remains their principal means of transition between Secondary/Tertiary and Higher Education. We hope that this book helps to change that.

Notes

1 Census dates refer to audits carried out in November, February and May to monitor funding.
2 Note that the Higher Education Academy is, at the time of writing, looking into developing a non-regulatory code of practice in teaching and learning for Higher Education.
3 No longer mandatory as of September 2013 but still considered necessary by employers.
4 Augmented reality (AR) is a live, direct or indirect, view of a physical, real-world environment whose elements are augmented by computer-generated sensory input such as sound, video, graphics or GPS data. With the help of advanced AR technology (e.g. adding computer vision and object recognition) the information about the surrounding real world of the user becomes interactive and digitally manipulable. Artificial information about the environment and its objects can be overlaid on the real world.
5 From 2014 the participation age will be raised to 17.

References

Allen, D. K. (2003). Organisational climate and strategic change in higher education: Organisational insecurity. *Higher Education, 46*, 61–92.

Anderson, L. W., and Krathwohl, D. R. (2000). *A taxonomy for learning, teaching, and assessing: A revision of Bloom's taxonomy of educational objectives*. New York: Longman.

Andrade, M. S. (2006). International students in English-speaking universities: Adjustment factors. *Journal of Research in International Education, 5*(2), 131–154.

Armitage, A., Bryant, R., Dunnill, R., Flanagan, K., Hayes, D., Hudson, A., Kent, J., Lawes, S., and Renwick, M. (2007). *Teaching and training in post-compulsory education* (3rd edn.). Maidenhead, Berks: Open University Press.

Atkinson, P. (1990). Creating cultural change. *Management Services, 34*(7), 6–10.

Atkinson, P., and Coffey, A. (1995). Realism and its discontents: The crisis of cultural representation in ethnographic texts. In B. Adam and S. Allen (Eds.), *Theorising culture* (pp. 103–139). London: UCL Press.

Ball, S. J. (1972). Self and Identity in the context of deviance: The case of criminal abortion. In R. Scott and J. Douglas (Eds.), *Theoretical perspectives on deviance* (pp. 158–186). New York: Basic Books.

Ball, S. (2008). *The education debate*. Bristol: Policy Press.

Barker, M., Child, C., Gallois, C., Jones, E., and Callan, V. (1991). Difficulties of overseas students in social and academic situations. *Australian Journal of Psychology, 43*, 79–84.

Bartram, B. (2007). The sociocultural needs of international students in Higher Education: A comparison of staff and student views. *Journal of Studies in International Education, 11*(2), 205–214.

Bartram, B. (2008). Supporting international students in Higher Education: Constructions, cultures and clashes. *Teaching in Higher Education, 13*(6), 657–668.

Beach, K. D. (1999). Consequential transitions: A sociocultural expedition beyond transfer in education. *Review of Research in Education, 24*, 101–139.

Beach, K. D. (2003). Consequential transitions: A developmental view of knowledge propagation through social organisations. In T. Tuomi-Gröhn and Y. Engeström (Eds.), *Between school and work: New perspectives on transfer and boundary crossing* (pp. 39–62). Amsterdam: Pergamon.

Belsey, C. (2002). *Post structuralism: A very short introduction*. Oxford: Oxford University Press.

Berk, L., and Winsler, A. (1995). *Scaffolding children's learning: Vygotsky and early childhood education*. Washington, DC: NAEYC.

Biggs, J. (1999). *Teaching for quality learning at university*. Buckingham: SRHE and Open University Press.

Bloom, B. S. (Ed.). (1956). *Taxonomy of educational objectives: The classification of educational goals*. New York, Toronto. Longmans.

Bostock, J. (2004). *An investigation and analysis of students' perceptions and attitudes to the integration of technology in the PCET classroom*. Unpublished MA Thesis, University of Greenwich, UK.

Bostock, J., and Wood, J. (2011). Andragogy vs. pedagogy: New approaches to teaching and learning. Paper presented at the Annual MMU Student Research Conference, Manchester Metropolitan University, 27 January.

Bostock, J., and Wood, J. (2012). *Teaching 14–19: A handbook*. London: Open University Press.

Boud, D. (2009). How can practice reshape assessment? In G. Joughin (Ed.), *Assessment, learning and judgement in Higher Education* (pp. 29–44). Dordrecht: Springer.

Bridges, W. (2009). *Managing transitions* (3rd edn.). Philadelphia, PA: Perseus Books.

Britzman, D. (2009). *The very thought of education: Psychoanalysis and the impossible professions*. New York: Sunny Press.

Brockbank, A., and McGill, I. (2012). *Facilitating reflective learning: Coaching, mentoring & supervision* (2nd edn.). London: Kogan Page.

Brookfield, S. (2005). *The power of Critical Theory for adult learning and teaching*. Maidenhead, Berks: Open University Press.

Brown, T. (2008). Desire and drive in researcher subjectivity: The broken mirror of Lacan. *Qualitative Inquiry, 14*(3), 402–423.

Bruner, J. (1966). *Toward a theory of instruction*. Cambridge, MA: Harvard University Press.

Busher, H. (2006). *Understanding educational leadership, people, power and culture*. London: Open University Press.

Claridge, M. T., and Lewis, T. (2005). *Coaching for effective learning*. Oxford: Radcliffe.

Clark, C. M. (1995). *Thoughtful teaching*. London: Cassell.

Conley, D. (2005). *College knowledge. What it really takes for students to succeed and what we can do to get them ready*. San Francisco, CA: Jossey-Bass.

Conley, D. (2007). *Toward a more comprehensive conception of college readiness*. Eugene, OR: Educational Policy Improvement Center.

Conley, D. (2008). Rethinking college readiness. *New Directions for Higher Education, Winter*(144), 3–13.

Connor, M., and Pokora, J. (2012). *Coaching & mentoring at work* (2nd edn.). Maidenhead, Berks: Open University Press.

Cooper, K., and Olson, M. R. (1996). The multiple 'I's' of teacher identity. In M. Kompf, W. R. Bond, D. Dworet, and R. T. Boak (Eds.), *Changing research and practice: Teachers' professionalism, identities and knowledge* (pp. 78–89). London/Washington, DC: The Falmer Press.

Cox, E. (2013). *Coaching understood*. London: Sage.

Crafter, S., and Maunder, R. (2012). Understanding transitions using a sociocultural framework. *Educational and Child Psychology, 29*(1), 10–18.

Day, C., Kington, A., Gu, Q., and Sammons, P. (2005). The role of identity in variations in teachers' work, lives and effectiveness. *British Educational Research Journal*.

Day, C., Kington, A., Stobart, G., and Sammons, P. (2006). The personal and professional selves of teachers: Stable and unstable identities. *British Educational Research Journal, 32*(4), 601–616.

Deal, T. E., and Kennedy, A. A. (1982). *Corporate cultures: Rites and rituals of organisational life*. Reading, MA: Addison Wesley.

DfES (2005). Functional skills support programme. Available from: http://www.dfes.gov.uk/14-19/. Accessed September 2013.

Dingwall, R., and Mcintosh, J. (1978). *Readings on the sociology of nursing*. London: Churchill Livingstone.

Downey, M. (2003). *Effective coaching* (2nd edn.). Independence, KY: Cengage Learning.

Duckworth, V., Wood, J., Dickinson, J., and Bostock, J. (2010). *Successful teaching practice in the lifelong learning sector*. Exeter, UK: Learning Matters.

Dunn, L., and Wallace, M. (2004). Australian academics teaching in Singapore: Striving for cultural empathy in innovations. *Education and Teaching International*, 41(3), 291–303.

Egan, G., and Cowan, M. (1979). *People in systems*. Monterey, CA: Brooks Cole.

Findlow, S. (2008). Accountability and innovation in Higher Education: A disabling tension? *Studies in Higher Education*, 33(3), 313–329.

Forman, E. A., Minick, N., and Addison Stone, C. (Eds.). (1993). *Contexts for learning*. New York: Oxford University Press.

Foucault, M. (1972). Cited in Robson, J. (2006). *Teacher professionalism in Further and Higher Education*. London: Routledge.

Francis, M., and Gould, J. (2009). *Achieving your PTLLS Award*. London: Sage.

Garvey, B., Stokes, P., and Megginson, D. (2008). *Coaching and mentoring*. London: Sage.

Gee, J. P. (2004). *Situated language and learning: A critique of traditional schooling*. London: Routledge.

Gee, J. P. (2005). *An introduction to discourse analysis: Theory and method*. Oxon: Routledge.

Ginnott, H. (1972). *Teacher and child: A book for parents and teachers*. New York: Harmony Books.

Glasser, W. (1988). *Choice theory in the classroom*. New York: Harper Perennial.

Goffman, M. (1959). Cited in Day, C., Kington, A., Stobart, G., and Sammons, P. (2006). The personal and professional selves of teachers: stable and unstable identities. *British Educational Research Journal*, 32(4), 601–616.

Gosling, D., and Moon, J. (2001). *How to use learning outcomes & assessment criteria*. London: SEEC.

Hanna, D. E. (2003). Cited in Drew, G. (2010). Issues and challenges in Higher Education leadership: Engaging for change. *The Australian Educational Researcher*, 37(3), 5.

Haynes, S. N., and Kaholokula, J. K. (2007). Behavioural assessment. In M. Hersen and A. M. Gross (Eds.), *Handbook of clinical psychology* (pp. 495–524). New York: John Wiley.

Hernandez-Martinez, P., Williams, J., Black, L., Davis, P., Pampaka, M., and Wake, G. (2011). Students' views on transitions from school to college mathematics: Rethinking 'transition' as an issue of identity. *Research in Mathematics Education*, 13(2), 119–130.

Holland, D., Lachicotte, W., Skinner, D., and Cain, C. (1998). *Identity and agency in cultural worlds*. Cambridge, MA: Harvard University Press.

Hou, J., Montgomery, C., and McDowell, L. (2011). Transition in Chinese–British Higher Education articulation programmes: Closing the gap between East and West? In J. Ryan (Ed.), *China's Higher Education reform and internationalisation* (pp. 104–119). London: Routledge.

Hyde, M. (2012). *The international student's guide to UK education: Unlocking university life and culture*. London: Routledge.

Institute for Learning (2006). *Realising the potential*. London: IFL.

Jackson, P. Z., and McKergow, M. (2007). *The solutions focus*. London: Nicholas Brealey International.

Joyce, B., and Showers, B. (2002). *Student Achievement through Staff Development* (3rd edn.). Alexandria, VA, USA: Association for Supervision and Curriculum Development.

Kolsaker, A. (2008). Academic professionalism in the managerialist era: A study of English universities. *Journal of Studies in Higher Education*, 33(5), 513–525.

Kotter, J. (2007). Cited in Drew, G. (2010). Issues and challenges in Higher Education leadership: Engaging for change. *The Australian Educational Researcher*, 37(3).

Lacan, J. (2006). Cited in Brown, T. (2008). Desire and drive in researcher subjectivity: The broken mirror of Lacan. *Qualitative Inquiry*, 14(3), 402–423.

Larcombe, W., and Malkin, I. (2008). Identifying students likely to benefit from language support in First-Year Law. *Higher Education Research and Development*, 27(4), 319–329.

Lefrancois, G. R. (1994). *Psychology for teaching* (8th edn.). Belmont, GA: Wadsworth.

Leonard, D., Pelletier, C., and Morley, L. (2003). *The experiences of international students in UK Higher Education: A review of unpublished research*. London: UKCOSA.

Lingfield, L. (2012). Professionalism in further education: Final report of the independent review panel. Department for Business, Innovation and Skills, London.

Lumby, J. (2001). *Managing Further Education*. London: Paul Chapman.

MacLure, M. (1993). Arguing for yourself: Identity as an organising principle in teachers' jobs and lives. *British Educational Research Journal*, 19(4), 311–322.

Mallinson, A. (2009). From school to further education: Student and teacher views of transition, support and drop-out. *Education and Child Psychology*, 26(1).

Martinez, P. (2001). *Improving student retention and achievement: What do we know and what do we need to find out?* London: LSDA.

Meador, D. (2013). Qualities of an effective teacher. Available at: blogspot.com/. . ./qualities-of-effective-teacher-ten.html

Megginson, D., and Clutterbuck, D. (2005). *Techniques for coaching and mentoring*. Oxford: Butterworth-Heinemann.

Mezirow, J. (2009). An overview on transformative learning. In K. Illeris (2009). *Contemporary theories of learning* (pp. 90–106). Abingdon, Oxon: Routledge.

Middlehurst, R. (2007). Cited in Drew, G. (2010). Issues and challenges in Higher Education leadership: Engaging for change. *The Australian Educational Researcher*, 37(3).

Minton, D. (2005). *Teaching skills in further and adult education* (3rd edn.). Thomson Learning.

Moon, J. (2002a). *How to use level descriptors*. London: SEEC.

Moon, J. (2002b). *The module & programme development handbook: A practical guide to linking levels, learning outcomes & assessment*. London: Kogan Page.

Nias, J. (1989). *Primary teachers talking*. London: Routledge.

Nuffield Review (2005). Pring, R. *et al*. *Education for all*. London: Routledge.

O'Donovan, B. (2008). Developing student understanding of assessment methods: A nested hierarchy of approaches. *Teaching in Higher Education*, 9(3), 325–335.

Overton, T. (2005). Writing learning outcomes: Advice on defining courses using an outcomes-based approach. The Higher Education Academy. Available from: http://www.heacademy.ac.uk/assets/ps/documents/primers/primers/writing_learning_outcomes.pdf

Passmore, J. (Ed.). (2010). *Excellence in coaching* (2nd edn.). London: Kogan Page.

Paton, G. (2012). 'Spoon-fed' students given tuition in basic skills at university. *The Telegraph*, 3 April. Available from: http://www.telegraph.co.uk/education/educationnews/9180982/Spoon-fed-students-given-tuition-in-basic-skills-at-university.html

Petty, G. (2004). *Teaching today* (3rd edn.). Cheltenham, Glos: Nelson Thornes.

Petty, G. (2010). *Teaching today* (4th edn.). Cheltenham, Glos: Nelson Thornes.

Postance, M. (2008). Planning for learning. In F. Fawbert (Ed.), *Teaching in PCE*. London: Continuum.

Price, M. (2012). *Assessment literacy: The foundation for improving student learning*. Wheatley: Oxford Brookes University.

Price, M., Handley, K., Millar, J., and O'Donovan, B. (2010). Feedback: All that effort but what is the effect? *Assessment and Evaluation in Higher Education*, 35(3), 277–289.

Price, M., Rust, C., O'Donovan, B., and Handley, K. (2012). *Assessment literacy: The foundation for improving student learning*. Oxford: The Oxford Centre for Staff and Learning Development.

Quality Assurance Agency. (2013). Quality code. Available from: http://www.qaa.ac.uk/AssuringStandardsAndQuality/quality-code/Pages/Quality-Code-Part-B.aspx

Race, P. (1995). 'Quality for some?' – what about the rest? *Journal of Further and Higher Education, 19*(1), 54–61.

Race, P. (2005). *Making learning happen – A guide for Post-Compulsory Education.* London: Sage.

Ramsden, P. (1998). Managing the effective university. *Journal of Higher Education Research and Development, 17*(3), 347–370.

Ramsden, P. (2003). *Learning to teach in Higher Education* (2nd edn.). London: Routledge Falmer.

Robson, J. (2006). *Teacher professionalism in Further and Higher Education.* London: Routledge.

Rogers, A. (2002). *Teaching adults.* Maidenhead, Berks: Open University Press.

Rogers, C. R. (1983). *Freedom to learn for the 80s.* Columbus, OH: Merrill.

Rogers, J. (2007). *Adults learning* (5th edn.). London: Open University Press.

Ryan, J. (2013). Comparing learning characteristics in Chinese and Anglophone cultures: Pitfalls and insights. In M. Cortazzi and L. Jin (Eds.), *Researching cultures of learning* (pp. 41–60). Basingstoke, Hants: Palgrave Macmillan.

Sachs, J., and Chan, C. (2003). Dual scaling analysis of Chinese students' conceptions of learning. *Educational Psychology, 23*(2), 181–192.

Sadler, D. R. (1987). Specifying and promulgating achievement standards. *Oxford Review of Education, 13*, 191–209.

Saravanamuthu, K., and Tinker, T. (2008). Ethics in education: The Chinese learner and post-Enron ethics. *Critical Perspectives on Accounting, 19*(2), 129–137.

Schein, E. H. (1985). *Organizational culture and leadership.* San Francisco, CA: Jossey-Bass.

Schon, D. A. (1991). *The reflective practitioner: How professionals think in action.* New York: Basic Books.

Scott, C. D., and Jaffe, D. T. (1995). *Managing change at work.* New Brunswick: Canadian Research Institute for Social Policy (CRISP) Publications.

Scott, G., Coates, H., and Anderson, M. (2008). *Learning leaders in times of change.* Sydney: Australian Teaching Council.

SEEC credit level descriptors. (2010). Available from: http://www.seec.org.uk/academic-credit/seec-credit-level-descriptors-2010

Senior, L. (2010). *The essential guide to teaching 14–19 diplomas.* Munich: Pearson Longman.

Sheridan, V. (2011). A holistic approach to international students, institutional habitus and academic literacies in an Irish third level institution. *Higher Education, 62*(2), 129–140.

Stapleton, M. (2001). *Psychology in practice.* Abingdon, Oxon: Hodder and Stoughton.

Starr, J. (2011). *The coaching manual* (3rd edn.). Harlow, Essex: Pearson Education.

Steed, E., and Sudworth, P. (1985). The humpback bridge. In R. Derricott (Ed.), *Curriculum continuity: Primary to secondary* (pp. 23–37). Berkshire,UK: NFER-Nelson.

Stradling, B., and Saunders, L. (1993). Differentiation in practice: Responding to the needs of all pupils. *Educational Research, 35*(2), 127–137.

Strathern, M. (Ed.). (2000). *Audit cultures: Anthropological studies in accountability, ethics and academy.* London: Routledge.

Stronach, I., Corbin, B., McNamara, O., Stark, S., and Warne, T. (2002). Towards an uncertain politics of professionalism: Teacher and nurse identities in flux. *Journal of Education Policy, 17*(1), 109–138.

Trotter, E. (2004). Enhancing the early student experience. Conference presentation, University of Salford.

Turner, E. (2012). The calm within the storm. *Coaching at Work, 7*(4), 8, 12–13.

Vizard, D. (2007). *How to manage behaviour in further education.* London: Sage.

Volet, S. (1999). Learning across cultures: Appropriateness of knowledge transfer. *International Journal of Educational Research*, *31*(7), 625–643.

Vrasidas, C., and McIsaac, M. S. (2001). Integrating technology in teaching and teacher education: Implications for policy and curriculum reform. *Educational Media International*, *38*(2/3), 127–132.

Vygotsky, L. S. (1978). *Mind in society: The development of higher psychological processes*. Cambridge, MA: Harvard University Press.

Walshe, J. (2009, updated 28 November 2012). Alarm as spoon-fed students can't cope at college. *The Independent*. Available from: http://www.independent.ie/irish-news/alarm-as-spoonfed-students-cant-cope-at-college-26543295.html

Wenger, E. (1998). *Communities of practice: Learning meaning and identity*. New York: Cambridge University Press.

Wheatley, M. J. (2003). *Change: The capacity of life*. San Francisco, CA: Jossey-Bass.

Whitmore, J. (2009). *Coaching for performance* (4th edn.). London: Nicholas Brealey.

Wolf, M. (2005). *Adulthood: New terrain*. San Francisco, CA: Jossey-Bass.

Wood, D., Bruner, J. S., and Ross, G. (1976). The role of tutoring in problem solving. *Journal of Child Psychology and Psychiatry*, *17*, 89–100.

Yorke, M. (2001). Formative assessment and its relevance to retention. *Higher Education Research and Development*, *20*(2), 115–126.

Zhou, Y., and Todman, J. (2008). Chinese postgraduate students in the UK: A two-way reciprocal adaptation. *Journal of International and Intercultural Communication*, *1*(3), 221–243.

Zittoun, T. (2006). *Transitions: Development through symbolic resources*. Greenwich, UK: Information Age Publishing.

Index

Page numbers in *italics* refer to tables.